THE QUANTUM REVOLUTION

Praise for *The Quantum Revolution: The Power to Transform*

"I've often said that we are living in one of the most interesting times. We are in the midst of the greatest revolution in history—a consciousness revolution. It eclipses the agricultural revolution and the industrial revolution. Michael Wayne's book, **The Quantum Revolution***, insightfully explains how we got to this point and offers steps we need to take to complete this revolution. This revolution will help transform the world into a more socially just, sustainable, open, connected and peaceful world. This book is hopeful but realistic and helps identify simple steps we can all take to ensure a bright future for the planet."* — **John Perkins**, *author*, **Confessions of an Economic Hit Man**

"Filled with jewels of wisdom boldly set in the crown of our future, this book gathers the best evolutionary thinking from the world's greatest philosophers and packs it together in one easily readable book. It guides you in the transformation of your own consciousness, and from that, into the quantum revolution that will take our world to the possibility of a thriving civilization." — **Anodea Judith, Ph.D.**, *author*, **The Global Heart Awakens**

"The Quantum Revolution *depicts a future world fully in tune with the interconnections of the* *underlying Quantum Reality. If evolution's Group Selection principles also hold true-- that altruistic systems always outcompete selfish ones— the world Michael Wayne predicts may come sooner than you think!"* — **Kurt Johnson Ph.D.**, *co-author*, **The Coming Interspiritual Age**

The Quantum Revolution:

The Power to Transform

Michael Wayne

*i*Think Books

The Quantum Revolution: The Power to Transform

Copyright © 2016 Michael Wayne
All rights reserved

ISBN-13: 978-0-9766797-3-8

Published by:
iThink Books
P.O. Box 393
Saratoga Springs, NY 12866
iThinkBooks@me.com

Printed in the United States of America
10987654321

Table of Contents

Introduction   9

Part 1: The Back Story
1. How Did We Get Here?	21
2. Where Are We Going?	35
3. What is Democracy?	40
4. Why a Quantum Revolution	48
5. The Blind Spot	56
6. Freeing Your Mind	61
7. Open and Closed	66
8. Getting Past Greed and Selfishness	72
9. Wall Street is a Mirror of All of Us	80
10. Personal/Quantum Transformation = Global Transformation	87
11. Becoming a More Complete Human Being	94

Part 2: The Keys to a Quantum Revolution
A. Personal/Quantum Transformation:
12. Low Density Lifestyle	105
13. Healing and Release	111
14. Self-Mastery	120

B. Societal Transformation:
15. Vision and Leadership — 129
16. Quantum Consciousness — 139
17. Creative Intelligence — 145
18. Conscious Evolution — 154
19. Presencing and Emergence — 162

Part 3: Viva la Revolucion!
20. Understanding Happiness: Lessons From Bhutan — 171
21. Towards An Open Future — 186
22. How to Start a Revolution — 202

Appendix
A. The Quantum Revolution Acronym — 209
B. The Components of a Quantum Revolution — 211

About the Author — 215

Introduction

"Peace is possible only when humans show compassion for all sentient beings. We must take responsibility for protecting life. Prayer is very good, and so is meditation. But it is not enough. We need to take action. Yes, we must act." — The Dalai Lama

"Never doubt that a small group of people of committed citizens can change the world. Indeed, it's the only thing that ever has." — Margaret Mead

"A revolution is coming—a revolution which will be peaceful if we are wise enough; compassionate if we care enough; successful if we are fortunate enough—But a revolution which is coming whether we will it or not. We can affect its character; we cannot alter its inevitability." — John F. Kennedy

A new future is emerging, and we have a golden opportunity to midwife it along. Make no mistake, though: there is much volatility in the air and much to be concerned about. Yet, the future belongs to those who see what is upon us.

An open future awaits: this is what is emerging, blossoming and coming to fruition. It is occurring technologically, culturally, economically, politically and spiritually—and this movement is finding its way into the mainstream.

And so, it may seem hard to fathom, but there are hopeful signs that the winds of a deep transformative change are collecting and beginning to reach a tipping point.

To paraphrase Buffalo Springfield in their song "For What It's Worth": *There's something happening here, and what it is is starting to become exactly clear.*

More people are starting to see or intuit this: as a dream, as a vision, and as a reality. This vision tells us that our diverse natures are like an outer shell that, when peeled away, show that no matter our cultural and religious differences, there is a thread that connects all of us, heart to heart and mind to mind.

At first this vision was considered a mystical experience, encountered by only a chosen few. But now, more and more people are awakening to this experience and insight. This experience is a dream, a vision, of a world of peace, of love, of a place where people act out of the greater good, where actions are based on how they impact future generations, and where things are valued if they give meaning.

This is not some pipe dream. It is a world in the making, because more people are awakening to this reality—and this awakening is creating a revolution. As of now, it's still somewhat of a quiet and simmering revolution, yet it's one that's been going on for quite a few years now in many realms, from health care, to politics, spirituality, science, the arts, environment, technology, food, business, and more. And the tide is turning, and if these movements are steered correctly, this could be one of the greatest social and cultural transformations in history, with the potential to create a peaceful, just, holistic, compassionate and sustainable society and world for a long time.

This movement is taking us towards an open future; I call this movement the Quantum Revolution. Over the course of the coming years, this Quantum Revolution is going to get louder, until the forces of change beckon it to become a tidal wave. This revolution will encompass change from the bottom up and top down, and from the inside out and outside in. It has the power to transform the world.

A Quantum Revolution signifies the awakening of the awesome power of heart and mind, for the betterment of the world. An awakened heart and mind allows people to vision more deeply and profoundly, a vision of what it takes to create a more peaceful, enlightened and sustainable world, and then create right action to help bring it to fruition.

This is an age where there is an incredible amount of polarization, with people caught up in black and white thinking to be for or against, and where fear and greed has become so overwhelming that it is threatening to cause immense economic, social, environmental and spiritual collapse.

To find a way to a more positive world will take more wisdom and more evolved ways of seeing. Our problems can't be solved from the level of thinking that created them. That way of thinking is limited, and the answers won't be found in that way. The Quantum Revolution will be both a revolution and an evolution—of thinking, of being, and of doing, in which we become more conscious, more aware, and more wise.

Throughout history, revolution and evolution has been a constant. From the dark ages through the Renaissance, from the Age of

Enlightenment to our current age, revolution, evolution and the ability to transform has been a consistent reality.

It often begins with a small number of people who commit themselves to change and transformation, and who know in their hearts and minds that what they are visioning is an idea whose time has come.

"The revolution will not be televised," said the poet Gil Scott-Heron. And indeed, this Quantum Revolution will not be televised; it will not play out on the nightly news or on CNN. It is happening around us, whether we are ready or not. Let's be ready.

There have been many revolutions throughout the course of history; some have succeeded, others have failed. But if it is just a political transformation, it is not enough, because as we have seen throughout the course of history, eventually in a political transformation, the oppressed ultimately become the oppressors.

Instead, it has to be a transformation of consciousness—in which there is a transformation of the individual—and a transformation of systems, in which people begin thinking and doing with greater clarity, greater awareness, greater love, and with a connection to the pulse of the universe, in order to move things along for the greater good.

A Quantum Revolution will create a world of peace; a world with a sane health care system that focuses on healing and wellness; a world of sustainable living; a world that focuses on the greater good; a world where people help one another without thinking "what's in it for me"; a world that measures economic growth by the happiness quotient of a nation's citizens; a world where people live to their fullest potential; a world where people can overcome their fears and take bold action; and a world of forward-thinking visionaries.

For millennia, this kind of world has been the collective imaginal dream of individuals and society. We now have it within our grasp to make this dream real. The Quantum Revolution will occur as more people move in this direction. Many of us are trying to change the world, in ways big and small. It may be personal change that you are working on, it may be societal change, or it may be a combination of the two.

It starts now. You have it in your power to do something and move things forward. In each of us is a seed that is hungry to be sparked. It is the desire for meaning, to live a life that has profound value not only to you but also to others. This hunger cannot be quenched: it needs to be watered, fed, nurtured, cultivated, and finally allowed to blossom. As it sprouts, it will call you, burn at you, demand from you. It will point you in the right direction. You cannot suppress it, because it cannot be squelched. Listen to it. It is the rivers of the pulse of the universe calling your name, asking you to join in with the Quantum Revolution, in order to help transform both yourself, your circle of loved ones, and the greater whole.

How do I know this is so? I can see the change happening all around me, as can any of you, if you just observe. In the field I work in, health care, I see the exponential growth of people wanting to become healthier by focusing on wellness, through acupuncture and Chinese medicine, and other holistic modalities. Along with that, the growth of the organic food industry is skyrocketing, as people demand higher quality foods, foods that are nurturing to health and environmentally sustainable. Yoga, that most ancient of Eastern traditions, has become so popular that it seems like there are yoga studios on every street corner. Meditation has become so immersed in the mainstream that businesses are incorporating it into the workplace; most recently, the World Bank had Thich Nhat Hanh lead a meditation workshop for employees. And the growing international interspiritual movement and network is bringing together many of the world's religions and spiritual practices in a coherent and unified way that is appealing to the large number of people who identify themselves as spiritual but not religious.

There are more books and media outlets now that are conveying the message of transformation, because people are desiring it, desiring lives that have meaning and purpose. And with the presence of the internet and social media, it is now possible for people to connect and societies to become more transparent and open as never before—we are truly becoming a global mind.

And we are becoming more tolerant and diverse as a global society. Who would have thought that a black man could become president of the United States? That was unthinkable not too long ago; now it is real.

According to surveys of cultural trends that have been done over the last 15 years, currently close to 30 percent of the U.S. population at this point is identified as interested in transformational change, and over 50 percent of the European population is identified in the same way.

The author Patricia Aburdene, in her book *Megatrends 2010*, forecast that over the next decade or so, 78 percent of the American population will more readily seek out meaning in their lives, and that this ethic will also be integrated into business.

Furthermore, Paul Hawken, in his book *Blessed Unrest: How the Largest Social Movement in History is Restoring Grace, Justice and Beauty to the World,* showed that there is a large and growing movement, comprised of over one million organizations, working towards bringing peace, harmony, sustainability and justice to our world.

I am asking you to join the Quantum Revolution, in order to help usher in a new, sustainable and transformative paradigm that is coming our way. You will be so glad you did.

This book, *The Quantum Revolution: The Power to Transform* advocates a revolution. In a non-polemical manner, it discusses how we got to the situation we're in now, and the steps to turn it around and how to get there. Through the lens of politics, sustainability, spirituality, personal transformation, technology, holism, psychology, quantum physics, and more, it lays out a map for getting where we need to go.

The Quantum Revolution lays out a hopeful and optimistic vision, but doesn't deny that we are at a crossroads that can push us into a deeper abyss. The more we work together, the more the positive vision that we know in our hearts to be true will become the world we and future generations will live in. There is a world waiting to be born anew, the seed of which we already carry within.

At the end of some of the chapters in this book, you will find a weblink and QR code that will take you to my website, www.DrMichaelWayne.com, where you will be able to view video interviews that I've done with various thought leaders in our society who are directly involved in transforming society into a more holistic, sustainable and enlightened world.

These interviews are from my video interview series "Interviews with the Leading Edge," and are in total alignment with the ideas in this book and also with the specific chapter that the link for each specific interview appears. I encourage you to watch each of the interviews, as they perfectly complement the ideas in this book.

Part One:
The Back Story

1. How Did We Get Here?

"The space of awareness is small, so that our personal distress looms large. But the moment you think of helping others, the mind expands and our own problems seem smaller." — The Dalai Lama

"The primary problem of the present era is that we're in between stories. The old story that bound Western culture, the story of reductionistic science and redemptive religion, is breaking down. It simply no longer explains the world we are experiencing or the changes that confront us." — Thomas Berry

"One does not need buildings, money, power, or status to practice the Art of Peace. Heaven is right where you are standing, and that is the place to train." — Morihei Ueshiba

How did we get to the place we're currently at, living in a world of such strife, of such disparities, and of such polarization? We are very good at discerning with our rational mind with the help of our analytical faculties, but not so good at integrating it with our heart. We can think and we can feel, but to combine the two doesn't always work.

We live disconnected from who we truly are, in a compartmentalized and non-integrated way. As we go through the day in disconnect mode, we live on autopilot, going through the motions on an everyday basis, day in and day out.

We may not think about the foods we eat and how they affect our health; or we may not think about our jobs and whether we are doing something that gives us meaning and purpose; we also may not think about our jobs and whether we are doing any harm to anyone with the work we do; we may not be thinking about our impact on the environment: the list goes on and on and on. We then compartmentalize the disconnect, in order to rationalize our actions: if we are not feeling well, we can go to the doctor and get some drugs to help us get well; if we get no fulfillment from our job then we will find fulfillment in our hobbies; if we are harming others with our job, we can ignore that because we are doing well financially, thanks to our job; and if our politicians don't care about the environment or the effects of climate change, why should I?

Because of this disconnect, we take no responsibility or ownership for our actions or how things affect us. It's someone else's fault, we tell ourselves, it has nothing to do with me—I'm just a victim of circumstances.

Yes, there are certain things beyond our control, but what we can control we can take ownership of. And yes, there are individuals with power, people who are living uber-disconnected lives—politicians and the corporate oligarchs behind them—that set a lot of the public and corporate policy, a policy that primarily benefits them; but that doesn't mean we have to live in a disconnected way, or accept it just because it is the status quo.

It is an unfortunate occurrence that corporate interest comes before the best interest of the public good. Granted, not all corporations think only about shareholder value: there is an entire movement, called conscious capitalism, in which the value of all stakeholders—the employee, the customer, the environment, and the shareholder—are taken into account. Yet, this movement towards conscious capitalism has not taken hold in the mainstream.

Ironically, the history of corporations is one that shows that at one time corporations were seen as a public trust, and a charter to have a corporation was only granted when a company showed that what they were doing would benefit the public.

But as time went on, and more and more disconnected people saw the benefits of corporations and how it could allow them to make a lot of money, pressure was put on government to allow anyone to incorporate. And with that, corporations were given free rein to do as they please.

An enlightened corporation might take their right to do business and make money seriously, and consider the ethics of all their actions; but the potent and combustible mix of unfettered free rein and the chance to make untold profits is too much for those who stay disconnected from themselves, which amounts to most of those running corporations. And for that matter, the entire financial system is based on disconnected thinking, in which the highest goal is to raise shareholder value by any means necessary.

The result of that is what we witness today: a paralysis to do anything while we witness financial meltdowns; the growing inequality of income; the continuing issue of climate change; the ever-increasing toxicity of our environment; the staggering cost of health care and its total blindness towards emphasizing wellness and true health; and more. All of this stems from a disconnect that causes us to act out self-absorbed behavior patterns like fear and greed, which are patterns that emanate from the primal reptilian brain, the part of the brain focused on survival.

If we were to act from a place where we weren't disconnected, it could still be from self-interest. But it would be an enlightened self-interest, as opposed to a self-absorbed one. There is nothing wrong with thinking about yourself and what furthers your own needs—the difference with enlightened self-interest is that when you think about what furthers your own needs, you take into consideration how it affects others. When this occurs, the disconnect starts to dissipate.

What does it look like when you move from self-absorbed behavior to something based on enlightened self-interest? I'd like to answer that question by giving examples through stories. Here are three stories, two that are works of fiction and one from real-life, that are examples of what a transformation from self-absorbed interest to enlightened self-interest looks like.

Remember Ebenezer Scrooge, as told in Charles Dickens' fable, "A Christmas Carol?" Scrooge had a singleminded goal—to make as much money as he could, even if it meant ruining the lives of others. And then one day he had an epiphany in which three ghosts came calling, and through their visitations, he came to realize that his life was meaningless, that he was an angry and spiteful old man who had been blind to how his actions affected others. His realization affected him in a most profound way—by the end of the story he had experienced a profound transformation that allowed him to open his heart and purse to others, and in the process, receive the love of those who had reviled him.

Or take the story of Phil Connors, from the film *Groundhog's Day*, a movie that has been hailed as one of the ten best American films ever, and one that some spiritual leaders have called "the most spiritual film of our time."

In *Groundhog's Day*, Bill Murray plays Phil Connors, a stressed out, self-centered, bitter and jaded television weatherman assigned to cover Groundhog's Day in Punxsutawney, PA. A blizzard keeps him in town that night, and he wakes up the next day to find out he is reliving Groundhog's Day again. And every night when he goes to bed, he arises the next morning to find out he is again reliving Groundhog's Day. This continues over and over, ad nauseam.

But Phil Connors is the only one who is reliving the day; he is the only one stuck in time. For everyone else, they begin anew at Groundhog's Day as if it never happened.

Connors then goes through a series of transitions, from first trying to use it to his advantage by learning secrets from the locals, seducing women, stealing money and getting piss drunk and driving around town. As the novelty wears off, and he sees the meaningless of his actions, he next kidnaps Phil the groundhog and kills himself and the groundhog. But again, he wakes up the next morning, still stuck back in Groundhog's Day.

And then a profound transformation of his character occurs, as he comes to realize the kind of horrible person he is—he is totally indifferent to anyone else but himself. He ceases his self-absorbed behavior patterns and cultivates the ability to deeply care about others. He also sincerely opens his heart and professes his love to his colleague Rita, who he always lusted after; Rita in response had only contempt for Phil Connors and his narcissistic, self-centered ways.

At the end of *Groundhog's Day*, Phil Connors and Rita unite in love. When they wake up in the morning together in bed, it is now Feb. 3: Groundhog's Day has ended and the time loop has broken. The two are together as a couple, and Phil Connors is a changed man, a man who has learned to live a more integrated life.

If fables aren't enough to sway you, let's take a look at a real-life story, that of Lee Atwater, an American political consultant and strategist to the Republican Party. He was an advisor to U.S. Presidents Ronald Reagan and George H. W. Bush and Chairman of the Republican National Committee. In addition, he was a master of distorting truths and spreading rumors, innuendos and outright lies to help his candidates, whether for local or national races, win office. He was described as "ruthless," "Ollie North in civilian clothes," and someone who "just had to drive in one more stake."

Atwater first rose to fame in 1980 in South Carolina, where he helped a Republican Congressional incumbent defeat his opponent with a number of underhanded tactics. He had the Senator from South Carolina at the time, Strom Thurmond, send a letter saying that the opponent would disarm America and turn it over to liberals and communists. At a press briefing, Atwater planted a "reporter" who rose and said, "We understand Tom Turnipseed [the opponent] has had psychotic treatment." Atwater later told the reporters off the record at the press conference that Turnipseed "got hooked up to jumper cables"—a reference to electroshock therapy.

Atwater's career apex was his work in 1988 as campaign manager for then Vice-President George H.W. Bush's successful presidential campaign. Atwater let fly unsubstantiated rumor after unsubstantiated rumor, including that Bush's opponent, Massachusetts governor Michael Dukakis, suffered from mental illness, and that his wife once burned an American flag in protest of the Vietnam War.

His worst and most hateful achievement were the ads he created about Willie Horton, a black man serving a life sentence in Massachusetts for first degree murder. Massachusetts had a law allowing for furloughs for prisoners, even for convicted murderers serving life sentences. While on furlough, Willie Horton kidnapped a couple and raped the woman. This was a heinous crime, no doubt, and Atwater played it for all it was worth, directly connecting Dukakis to Horton and with it, blaming Dukakis for Horton's crime. There were also racial undertones to the ad, in which white voters were cautioned to be very afraid of black men.

Atwater's inclusion of the racial card was no mistake. It was part of the Republican party's Southern Strategy. Atwater spelled it out in an interview he gave in 1981:

> You start out in 1954 by saying, "Nigger, nigger, nigger." By 1968 you can't say "nigger"—that hurts you. Backfires. So you say stuff like forced busing, states' rights and all that stuff. You're getting so abstract now [that] you're talking about cutting taxes, and all these things you're talking about are totally economic things and a byproduct of them is [that] blacks get hurt worse than whites. And subconsciously maybe that is part of it. I'm not saying that. But I'm saying that if it is getting that abstract, and that coded, that we are doing away with the racial problem one way or the other. You follow me—because obviously sitting

around saying, "We want to cut this," is much more abstract than even the busing thing, and a hell of a lot more abstract than "Nigger, nigger."

Atwater's tactics have been used many times over since the 1988 presidential campaign, and in all cases the strategy consists of distorting the truth by playing with visceral issues that play on peoples emotions. The issues that are used are called wedge issues, because they focus on things that push people apart and put a wedge between them, preying on the baser human survival instincts of fear, ignorance and hatred.

Atwater did not live to see his legacy unfold. He died in 1991, at the age of 40, a year and a half after having a brain tumor diagnosed. In the last chapter of his life, from his cancer diagnosis to his death, Atwater became a changed man, much like Ebeneezer Scrooge and Phil Connors.

After his cancer was discovered, Atwater issued a number of public and written letters to individuals to whom he had been opposed during his political career. In a letter to Tom Turnipseed dated June 28, 1990, he stated, "It is very important to me that I let you know that out of everything that has happened in my career, one of the low points remains the so-called 'jumper cable' episode," adding, "my illness has taught me something about the nature of humanity, love, brotherhood and relationships that I never understood, and probably never would have."

In a February 1991 article for *Life* magazine, Atwater wrote:

> My illness helped me to see that what was missing in society is what was missing in me: a little heart, a lot of brotherhood. The 1980s were about acquiring—acquiring wealth, power, prestige. I know. I acquired more wealth, power, and prestige than most. But you can acquire all you want and still feel empty. What power wouldn't I trade for a little more time with my family? What price wouldn't I pay for an evening with friends? It took a deadly illness to put me eye to eye with that truth, but it is a truth that the country, caught up in its ruthless ambitions and moral decay, can learn on my dime. I don't know who will lead us through the 1990s, but they must be made to speak to this spiritual vacuum at the heart of

American society, this tumor of the soul.

Lee Atwater's approach, of breeding and inciting hate, fear and ignorance, is a zero-sum game in which one person wins at the expense of another. Sure, the winner gains the glory and spoils of victory, but at what price? They gain power, wealth, prestige: but how many people have been harmed to achieve it? Is that the kind of society we want?

Unfortunately, this is the kind of society we have. And it no longer works—it actually never worked, but we are at a point in time where we can no longer afford to even have it as part of the equation.

We can't keep going on the winner-takes-all carousel, because that means there are also losers, people who suffer so that others may have material gains. In sports we want winners and losers clearly spelled out—that's part of the fun of sports. But in real life, it doesn't work. It has to be changed to a collaborative model, where everyone is a winner.

We are a busy, information-rich culture, but something has been lost: our hearts. We are drowning in information but starved for knowledge. We are full of technical know-how but lacking in wisdom and intuition. This is the ultimate disconnect.

2. Where Are We Going?

"The arc of the universe is long, but it bends towards justice." — Martin Luther King, Jr.

"Every few hundred years in western history there occurs a sharp transformation. Within a few short decades, society—its worldview, its basic values, its social and political structures, its arts, its key institutions—rearranges itself... We are currently living through such a time." — Peter Drucker

"The revolution is not an apple that falls when it is ripe. You have to make it fall." — Che Guevara

We are becoming more and more aware that the current path we are on is not sustainable. Crises in health care, economics, politics, international relations, banking and finance, environment, energy, education, and human services indicate that our system is broken.

We simply can't keep going the way we've been going. It just won't work as presently constituted. We've reached a logical endgame. Sure, we can keep trying to patch things up, putting band-aids on the wounds of the sick patient. But that doesn't lead to a cure.

And we can't rely on our politicians to lead us through this. The political system is broken, corrupted by the influence of moneyed interests. There are a few politicians who have the integrity to do the right thing and put the interests of people first, but the vast majority of politicians are doing the bidding of the corporations and individuals with the deepest pockets.

To find our way to a better world, we have to embrace a larger perspective, a global one, where we see things from a holistic viewpoint in which we integrate our minds and hearts, and in the process develop and cultivate a more evolved consciousness.

You could call this holistic viewpoint a non-dualistic, non-dogmatic, and non-rigid perspective; the best way to recognize it is by the ability to see and understand from multiple perspectives. To arrive at this destination, we must cultivate the ability to be present at all times. Logic alone will not suffice in a holistic viewpoint. We need to develop a combination of logic and intuition, analytical intelligence and emotional intelligence, objective and subjective, quantified and qualified.

By balancing our logical capabilities with a touch of the mystic, we bring new awareness to problem solving by which we can enter into the recesses of space to discover otherwise inaccessible answers. This is what all the great scientists, inventors, thinkers, and artists have done throughout time: extraordinary insights come from a place beyond our everyday world—from a place of knowing beyond knowing, from a place of deep intuitive presence.

We need to put the emphasis on living that is sustainable, holistic, respectful, collaborative and regenerative. There is nothing wrong with making a truckload of money, but it needs to be based on a model that is not a zero-sum game.

The recent economic downturn was caused by letting banks do whatever they wanted, tax cuts for those who didn't need any more breaks, and ill-thought out wars. All of these actions were based on thinking predicated on a zero-sum game where one person wins and another loses, as opposed to a collaborative model.

Since the New York Stock Exchange began business in earnest in the 19th century, it has been seen that letting banks do what they want has been the cause of numerous stock market panics, crashes and economic downturns. Yet, elected officials, funded by banking interests, are always glad to rescind laws and safeguards that protect the general public from predatory banks and financial firms who have but one general goal: use money to make more money. And in their quest to make more money, banks and financial firms become reckless in their pursuit of the profits, even if it upends the entire economy.

If we work from a collaborative model, banks would not have been given carte blanche to do what they want. Laws would not have been rescinded, meaning more checks and balances would have been in place.

There are many politicians, who on hearing talk about a system based on a more collaborative (and equitable) model, cry out "socialism" or "class warfare." Politicians like these are from the Lee Atwater school of politics, of using less than ethical tactics to get what they want, or need. And generally what they want and need is to protect the interests of their monied sponsors.

A collaborative model is pure democracy in action. It is about everyone working together so that everyone can succeed in a way that also promotes the greater good. Sure, some will succeed more than others, as well they should, if they have added something of value to our society. But the hope is that as some succeed, others can also succeed, if even to a lesser degree, and as this happens, the greater good is achieved.

Benjamin Franklin once said, "We must, indeed, all hang together, or assuredly we shall all hang separately." And President John F. Kennedy said, "Those programs which make life better for some of our people will make life better for all of our people. A rising tide lifts all the boats."

We are all interconnected, in a circle of life. When one succeeds, everyone succeeds. That is the purpose of democracy.

Watch: an Interview with John Perkins, author of the bestselling book, *Confessions of an Economic Hit Man*, from the video interview series, "Interviews with the Leading Edge."
http://drmichaelwayne.com/leadingedge/john-perkins/

3. What is Democracy?

"We have frequently printed the word Democracy. Yet I cannot too often repeat, that it is a word the real gist of which still sleeps, quite unawakened...It is a great word, whose history, I suppose, remains unwritten, because that history has yet to be enacted. It is, in some sort, younger brother of another great and often used word, Nature, whose history also waits unwritten." — Walt Whitman

"Government of the people, by the people, for the people, shall not perish from the Earth."
— Abraham Lincoln

"The spirit of democracy is not a mechanical thing to be adjusted by abolition of forms. It requires change of heart." — Mohandas Gandhi

What is democracy? To this day, it is still an evolving and developing form. The term democracy first appeared in ancient Greek political and philosophical thought in the Greek city-state of Athens, led by Cleisthenes, who established what is generally held as the first democracy in 507 BCE; Cleisthenes is referred to as "the father of Athenian democracy."

The Athenian philosopher Plato contrasted democracy, the system of "rule by the governed," with the alternative systems of monarchy (rule by one individual), oligarchy (rule of the wealthy) and timocracy (rule by an elite class valuing honor as opposed to wealth).

Although democracy has its formal origins in Ancient Greece, democratic practices have been evident in earlier societies including Mesopotamia, Phoenicia and India. Other cultures and geographical regions since Greece, such as Ancient Rome, Europe, and North and South America, have significantly contributed to the evolution of democracy. The concept of representative democracy arose largely from ideas and institutions that developed during the European Middle Ages and the Age of Enlightenment and in the American and French Revolutions.

While there is no universally accepted definition of democracy, equality and freedom have both been identified as important characteristics of democracy since ancient times. These principles are reflected in all citizens being equal before the law and having equal access to legislative processes. For example, in a representative democracy, every vote has equal weight, no unreasonable restrictions can apply to anyone seeking to become a representative, and the freedom of its citizens is secured by legitimized rights and liberties, which are generally protected by a constitution.

At its core, democracy signifies the right of people to be free, in order for them to evolve towards their greatest potential in tandem with promoting the greater good. This understanding sees democracy as not only a political system but as an ideal, an aspiration, intimately connected to and dependent upon a picture of what it is to be human —of what it is a human should be to be fully human.

In this definition, the goal of a democratic society is to help every person realize, to the best of their abilities, their aspirations, dreams and goals. There is a certain amount of self-reliance that is needed for a person to realize their abilities, and a certain amount of help from the community. Both individual and community play an important role in the development of an individual and their ability to be the best they can be, and as always, it is set within the context of the greater good for all.

In the quote by Walt Whitman that appears at the beginning of this chapter, he says that democracy is "a word the real gist of which still sleeps, quite unawakened...It is a great word, whose history, I suppose, remains unwritten, because that history has yet to be enacted."

Whitman then compares the word democracy with the word nature, and says that democracy is the "younger brother of another great and often used word, Nature, whose history also waits unwritten."

What does the great bard Whitman mean by this? Democracy is an ideal, a concept that is still in its ideological infancy. The essence of democracy is to help a person aspire to their greatest potential while helping to promulgate the greater good, and that we all are interconnected in this mission.

To achieve this purest interpretation of democracy, it takes an enlightened perspective, one that integrates self-interest with the best interests of community, society and the world. To reach this ideal, it requires, as Gandhi said, "A change of heart."

Democracy should be love in action, in which we all work together to better humanity. Whitman compared democracy to nature, saying they were related, and also pointed out how nature's history is also unwritten.

The tendency is to fight and conquer nature, to see it as the enemy. But nature is not unlike the Tao; it is something we need to learn to live in harmony with. You can't fight nature, because nature will fight back. Nature is like water; it can't be easily stopped or dammed up because it needs to flow, to be free, to find its way. Humans and nature have a symbiotic relationship: in order to succeed, each needs the other.

We can't destroy nature in the name of control and manipulation, as if nature was put on this earth for our subjugation, manipulation, perversion and domination. If anything, humans were put on this earth for nature's domination. But nature has always been willing to work collaboratively with humans. Sadly, humans haven't been willing to return the favor in kind.

Such is the same with democracy. Democracy can't be restrained, nor tethered. It needs to be free—that is the essence of democracy. Humans need to work collaboratively with democracy: help each other be free, help each other aspire to their greatest potential, help each other benefit the greatest good, so that all can succeed. We shouldn't look to subjugate, manipulate or dominate anyone. To do that entails the propagation of lies and distortions.

We don't need that. It's toxic and harmful, and suppresses the greater aspirations and dreams of people by stirring up their fears and anxieties, and pits one group of people against another. This kind of behavior is usually predicated on greed and fear, and, at the cost of promoting the greater good, it promotes the good of only specific groups. We have so much in common with one another, yet we are pushed in a direction that causes us to focus on our baser instincts, which are the wedge issues that drive us apart.

We need people committed to Truth, people who are integrated of body, mind and soul, who have a vision of a better way, and can inspire others to go in that direction. We can't solve our problems using the same tactics, words and actions that have created our problems. As Albert Einstein said, "Problems can never be solved from the level of thinking that created them."

And as Martin Luther King, Jr. said, "Darkness cannot drive out darkness; only light can do that. Hate cannot drive out hate; only love can do that."

The ideas of the founding fathers of the United States were borne out of the Age of Enlightenment, an era in which humans shook off the constraints of religious dogma and superstitious thinking to value reason, logic and the higher cognitive powers of the intellect.

Out of this era came new perspectives in science, culture, economics, philosophy and politics. Monarchies were toppled, and the separation of church and state was instituted. By doing this democracy was allowed to flourish, a democracy that was not beholden to any one religion, and especially was not ruled by any religious dogma.

The beginnings of democracy in the modern era took hold in the 18th century, first with the American Revolution. This led to a sea change around the world, by demonstrating that government could be of the people, by the people, and for the people. Democracy was truly an offspring of an enlightened worldview.

Now, this ideal called democracy is being manipulated, distorted and perverted to a most severe degree; in the U.S., democracy is transforming into an oligarchy and a corporatocracy. In order to find a way back towards this ideal, to bring democracy back into balance, it will take a new enlightened worldview. If you call what we need a New Age of Enlightenment, you wouldn't be wrong, although I prefer calling it a Quantum Revolution.

Watch: an Interview with Peter Yarrow, musician with Peter, Paul and Mary, from the video interview series, "Interviews with the Leading Edge." http://drmichaelwayne.com/leadingedge/peter-yarrow/

4. Why a Quantum Revolution?

"The greatest revolution in our generation is that of human beings, who by changing the inner attitudes of their minds, can change the outer aspects of their lives." — Marilyn Ferguson

"It's not that we need to form new organizations. It's simply that we have to awaken to new ways of thinking. I believe it makes no sense to spend a lot of time attacking the current realities. It is time to create the new models that have in them the complexity that makes the older systems obsolete. And to the extent that we can do that, and do that quickly, I think we can provide what will be necessary for a major breakthrough for the future." — Don Beck

"To change the world, you have to change people's minds." — Daniel Quinn

It's not enough to advocate change, unless there is also a change in people's minds, in the way they think. We have to awaken to new ways of thinking. The old ways are not working, because they are incomplete.

In order to awaken to this new way of thinking, all of us need to become more connected, integrated and in alignment with our truth, which allows us to operate from our highest Self. When this occurs we can see with our mind's eye and understand how our actions may impact future generations.

A Quantum Revolution is predicated on using the greater part of the mind's capabilities, in order to think at a higher, broader and deeper level. To do so entails redoing the way we are programmed to think and act.

The way we are programmed to think and act is based on a very rigid model of absolutism, one in which we subscribe to an either/or pattern—either I am right and you are wrong, or you are right and I am wrong, although most times I will stick to my guns and believe that I am right and you are wrong. The tendency is to hold onto beliefs, no matter what, even when faced with evidence that shows that what we believe flies against the face of facts.

Belief patterns can become so ingrained in the mind and body that they become entrenched, and in the process, toxic to your well-being. Yet if it allows you to operate within a safe comfort zone, then it's easier to stick with what you know, even if wrong, then to step outside yourself and embrace something that is foreign.

The human mind treats a new concept the way the body treats a strange protein—it rejects it. By doing so, the mind can then start to twist and distort the way it sees things in order to operate at its normal capability, which will lead someone operating this way to see the world through a very skewed lens.

The body can reject strange proteins, but when a person's immune system isn't functioning properly, the body starts seeing all types of things introduced into the body as strange proteins and rejects them—this is the genesis of auto-immune disease. Simple things that are part of nature, such as tree and flower pollen, or grasses, or food substances like wheat and oats, can then create harmful reactions in the body, because the immune system turns on itself and attacks these natural substances as foreign invaders.

The reason this occurs is because the immune system is compromised in some way, and has become a hostile host. It isn't capable of accepting these guests as benign, and instead sees them as threats to its very existence.

The same is true with the way we think. It's easier to attack a new idea or concept as foreign and a threat to your existence and way of being, than to accommodate it and allow it to open your way of thinking to new horizons and boundaries.

There is a saying in Zen that "when one person transmits a falsehood, myriad people transmit it as the truth." You can always find support for your point of view, even if it's based on a falsehood, rather than question your belief system and change the way you view things. To do so requires flexibility of mind and body.

A little more than 100 years ago there was a momentous and radical scientific revolution that occurred—the advent of quantum mechanics. This breakthrough was the original Quantum Revolution, the ramifications of which continue to evolve in our present day. Its emergence called into question everything that had been believed up to that point and it changed the understanding of how the universe, and life, functions.

The pioneering and visionary scientists behind the discoveries of quantum mechanics stared at the laws of nature unfolding in front of their eyes and realized that what they were uncovering upended all the cherished beliefs of science. At first these newly realized laws seemed to make no sense, but in time what seemed counterintuitive became irrefutable. Scientists began to sound like mystics as they attempted to explain the findings of quantum mechanics:

> "If quantum mechanics hasn't profoundly shocked you, you haven't understood it yet."—Niels Bohr

> "In the beginning there were only probabilities. The universe could only come into existence if someone observed it. It does not matter that the observers turned up several billion years later. The universe exists because we are aware of it."
> —Martin Rees

> "After you learn quantum mechanics you're never really the same again." —Steven Weinberg

> "When you change the way you look at things, the things you look at change."
> — Max Planck

"The doctrine that the world is made up of objects whose existence is independent of human consciousness turns out to be in conflict with quantum mechanics and with facts established by experiment."
— Bernard d'Espagnat

"It is often stated that of all the theories proposed in this century, the silliest is quantum theory. In fact, some say that the only thing that quantum theory has going for it is that it is unquestionably correct."— Michio Kaku

"Quantum physics thus reveals a basic oneness of the universe."—Erwin Schroedinger

This original Quantum Revolution showed that the universe is a living, breathing entity, full of consciousness and information, and that matter only makes up a very small component of the universe. It opened doors of understanding and perception in many domains by showing that an invisible thread interconnects us, and that consciousness and energy are the core components of this matrix.

Consciousness, energy, and information lie at the heart of the universe. Our universe is a living energy universe, one that is a knowing participant in the patterns that make up the complexities of life. Things continually change and evolve in an interactive conversation in which the macrocosm communicates with the microcosm to set the course of direction.

Our universe, our world, and our way of life is a blend of the scientific and spiritual—the tangible and the intangible. When the scientific and spiritual are combined, a higher, deeper, and broader logic and way of knowing, one that encompasses the intuitive understandings that the original Quantum Revolution brought forth, emerges.

Just as the scientific breakthroughs of the original Quantum Revolution opened the doors of perception, the new Quantum Revolution is propelling us through these doors into new and enlightened ways of being, thinking, and doing. By combining the scientific with the spiritual, new awareness about ourselves, our community, and the world are emerging, along with sustainable and enlightened solutions to the world's problems.

The new Quantum Revolution will lead to a more enlightened mindset, because it will lead to changing the very core of our existence—it will change people's minds.

Watch: an Interview with Anodea Judith, author of the book *The Global Heart Awakens*, from the video interview series, "Interviews with the Leading Edge." http://drmichaelwayne.com/leadingedge/anodea-judith/

5. The Blind Spot

"There's nothing more difficult than changing yourself." — Buddhist saying

"We are disturbed not by what happens to us, but by our thoughts about what happens." — Epictetus

"Beliefs can easily cause us to become blind to the obvious." — Dean Radin

Physiologically, the blind spot is a visual phenomenon. It is the location on the retina known as the optic disk, where the optic nerve fibers exit the back of the eye. Because there are no cones or rods at this point on the retina, there is a very small gap in the visual field.

Researchers have proposed a number of different explanations as to why we do not notice this blind spot. Some suggest that the opposite eye compensates for the missing visual information. One of the most commonly accepted theories is that the brain actually fills in the missing information using visual cues in the environment.

In a vehicle, a blind spot is an area around the vehicle that cannot be directly observed by the driver while at the controls, under existing circumstances.

Psychologically, the blind spot is aspects of your personality that are hidden from your view. It is the number one impediment in your life, because it obstructs your ability to live from your truth and to be in alignment with your highest Self. When you are not in alignment with who you truly are, then the disconnect takes place and you are incapable of actions that serve the greatest good, because the only person you care to serve is yourself and your thoughts are focused only on furthering your own needs.

The blind spot is the things we think and do unconsciously, based on our past patterns, habits and programming. To become aware of the blind spot takes a tremendous amount of self-awareness and courage, because you have to be willing to face yourself head-on.

When you walk around unaware of your blind spot, you end up sabotaging yourself and unconsciously getting in your own way. The blind spot can also derail your life and seriously diminish the possibilities for achieving your dreams and living a more fulfilled and integrated life.

It's easy to know when the blind spot is being activated—when your buttons get pushed and triggered, your mind then starts to spin out of control and operates from a place beyond your conscious perception: the blind spot.

A case in point of a blind spot is the need to always be right. This usually comes across as always being unwilling to listen to contrary points of view or, when challenged, to become defensive or to make others the scapegoats for your failures and mistakes. A negative consequence is a breakdown in honest communication between yourself and others.

Denial is an integral tool to staying in the dark about your blind spots, and allows you to maintain your belief system no matter the costs. Denial isn't the inability to perceive information, but the ability to perceive information while automatically refusing to allow it into consciousness.

We build up these blind spots because of information that is so troubling, so frightening, or so opposed to what we believe that to absorb it would shatter our view of ourselves and the world.

We usually project our blind spots onto others through a transference process that psychologists call reaction formation. A reaction formation results in a strong negative or positive reaction or stance and involves unconsciously transforming an unacceptable or undesirable impulse into its opposite. That is why those who are the most intolerant of others—because of race, class status, morals, gender, or sexual orientation—often have a blind spot that they are projecting onto others.

How can we ever come together as a people and work together from a more enlightened and integrated place, if we allow ourselves to become controlled by our blind spot? The blind spot causes us to be ruled by bigotry, hatred, fear and greed, and to take our cues from demagogic politicians and other thought leaders built from the same cloth.

We live in a world of diversity, and there is much that shows how different each one of us is. Yet at the same time, there is more that unites us than separates us.

In 1779, the English poet and clergyman John Newton wrote an astonishing and profound song that spoke of his own awakening. In 1748, while working as a slave trader on a ship, he experienced the light of awareness that shined on his blind spot. He went on to spell it out right from the first chorus of his song, "Amazing Grace":

> Amazing Grace, how sweet the sound,
> That saved a wretch like me.
> I once was lost but now am found,
> Was blind, but now I see.

Newton realized the immorality of what he was doing, and after that stopped his work as a slave trader and became an abolitionist.

We all have emotional blind spots. They are easy to recognize in someone else. As we become more self-aware, we can more fully recognize our own blind spots. And as we do so, we can know ourselves better and become more enlightened as to who and what we are.

How do you know what your blind spots are? It takes effort to do so, but becoming fully conscious of your perceptions—simply feeling what you feel and knowing what you know—is the very definition of awakening. It creates a virtually indestructible foundation for lasting relationships, successful endeavors, and inner peace. Hunting down your blind spots is a bumpy adventure, but it can lead to sublime destinations.

6. Freeing Your Mind

*"You tell me it's the institution,
Well, you know
You better free you mind instead"* — The Beatles

"Ever since the human race first learned to wonder, men and women have been haunted by this irrepressible dream: that the limits of human ability lie beyond the boundaries of the imagination; that every human being uses only a fraction of his abilities; that there must be some way for everyone to achieve far more of what is truly theirs to achieve. History's greatest prophets, mystics and saints have dreamed even more boldly, saying that all men are somehow one with God." — George Leonard

"Dream no small dreams for they have no power to move the hearts of men." — Goethe

We have such immense capacity to vision, to think in the largest way possible, to dream a large dream. Yet we hold ourselves back—out of fear, complacency, and an inability to get past our comfort zone.

What would happen if you were to dare to dream, to embrace your greater capacity to vision? You then would be capable of living a more fulfilling life, one in which you could have your radiance shine onto the world. You would also then be able to dream of a greater and more positive world for all, and put that dream into action.

Dare to dream: to do so, we have to free our minds.

The answers are already out there, waiting for us to see, feel, touch and understand them. Albert Einstein once said that if he had an hour to come up with an answer, the first 59 minutes would be spent formulating the question, and once that was done, the answer would come.

All the great discoveries—scientific, technological, creative, cultural, social, or even spiritual—truly weren't discoveries, because the answer was already present. It was more a matter of humans being able to grasp the answer, by developing the language, cognitive capabilities, intuition, wisdom, insight, and boldness and vision to see the solution.

When Isaac Newton formulated his theory of gravity, he didn't discover it. Gravity was already there, it was a fact of life and a law of nature. But he was able to grasp it, see it, and understand it enough to language it. The same can be said of Einstein's development of the theory of relativity, or the development of quantum physics, or the invention of the Apple computer, or the development of jazz and rock and roll, or the conceiving of democracy—the list is endless.

All these inventions, ideas, and breakthroughs, all of which caused seismic shifts in the way we think and act, were not things that came out of nowhere. They were there, all around us. It was just a matter of humans developing the capability to grasp it, even if it was just a seed of an idea at first.

The genesis of breakthrough ideas is always a collaborative effort, even if the people involved are separated by great distances nor know of one another. One person may have the germ of an idea come to them, and then that seed enters into the noosphere, a term, developed by Pierre Teilhard de Chardin, the French philosopher, Jesuit priest, paleontologist and geologist, that denotes the sphere of human thought. Teilhard de Chardin stated that the noosphere emerges through and is constituted by the interaction of human minds.

So when someone comes up with an idea, the seed begins to carry into the noosphere, and the process of germination begins. The idea can then enter the minds of others who are tuned into the idea, and this can then become the collaborative effort that leads to the breakthrough.

Each of the people visioning the idea are tapping into a greater mind, something that can be called, for lack of a better term, Universal Mind, or the Field (short for Quantum Field). The Universal Mind is where the answers exist, and where, when we develop the capacity for seeing, intuiting and understanding, we can find them.

Contrary to popular opinion, creation and innovation is usually not predicated on one person having the grand vision, where everything comes to him or her in a flash and then they are able to configure the answer. Usually, the seed comes to a person, and as they contemplate it, it enters into the noosphere. From there, over time, the answers start to unfold.

To allow this process to happen, a person truly has to free their mind and accept that they may not be able to understand what it is they are grasping. This takes the ability to experience a state of deep knowing, of allowing for uncertainty to be part of the equation.

This is not always easy, because we are programmed to expect answers. But the development of ideas usually doesn't follow a smug path. They emerge and unfold, evolving over time until they become clear.

And so it is with the answers we are all looking for that can help lead us to a more positive and sustainable future. The answers are there, they are just waiting for humans to cultivate the ability to see and grasp them.

We all know what we want. We just have to formulate the question so that we can have the answer emerge.

Dare to dream: we just have to free our minds. And to do so, we have to let go of the need to know with certainty what the answers are. Instead we have to embrace the deep knowing, and know that through collaboration and the evolution of the noosphere, the answers will start to unfold.

7. Open and Closed

"Every human being on the face of the earth has a steel plate in his head, but if you lie down now and then and get still as you can, it will slide open like elevator doors, letting in all the secret thoughts that have been standing around so patiently, pushing the button for a ride to the top. The real troubles in life happen when those hidden doors stay closed for too long." — Sue Monk Kidd

"The world is full of people who have never, since childhood, met an open doorway with an open mind." — E.B. White

"He who can no longer pause to wonder and stand rapt in awe, is as good as dead; his eyes are closed." — Albert Einstein

Open systems succeed, closed systems fail. This is one of the key concepts of the Quantum Revolution.

A system is anything comprised of complexity, be it individual or group. An open system is where there is a degree of openness that allows for the cross-pollination of ideas—it is holistic in nature. A closed system is rigid and mechanistic, and continues doing the same thing and operating in the same way, even if the approach has proven to not work.

Open systems are based on an infinite and expanding universe, one that continually evolves and grows. A closed system is based on finiteness, and does its best to resist growth.

Closed systems may ultimately fail, but the vast majority of people and organizations function that way. Yet, we are rapidly moving into an open future, and so, it's best if we all get on the bus.

In a closed system organization, there is a rigid hierarchy that controls every aspect of the organization under its domain. This hierarchy demands opaqueness and secrecy to cloud its operation, and believes it can dictate to the public what the public's needs and wants are.

In an open system organization, the hierarchy is fluid and looser. There may be one person who sits atop the chain of command, or it could be a different structure altogether. An open system is more egalitarian, and exchanges material, energy, capital and information with the public, in order to work in partnership with the public.

The new digital economy is a demonstration

of the transition occurring from closed to open systems. The music business, for example, was traditionally owned and operated by record companies, who were able to control the entire chain of music distribution, from having the musicians under their control, to promoting the music and controlling distribution.

Now, musicians can, if they so choose, release their music directly to the public through the internet, and by so doing, bypass the record companies. People can download entire CDs, or individual songs. The entire music business has changed and become more open, giving musicians a direct pipeline to their fans, and giving them the opportunity to develop their fanbase in an organic, grassroots way.

The organization WikiLeaks is another example of an open system, and of what this type of system can do to a closed system. WikiLeaks publishes submissions of private, secret, and classified media from anonymous news sources, news leaks, and whistleblowers. Their aim is to take the private, secret and opaque dealings of governments and government agencies and make them transparent by shining attention on what goes on behind closed doors. Governments that are not representing the best interests of its citizenry but instead the best interests of those with the access, through their wallets, to the inner chambers of power, work best when they implement policy without the full knowledge of their citizenry. By releasing information that allows the general public to know what their government officials are doing, WikiLeaks is striving for more accountability on the individuals in government who make decisions that can impact people all around the world.

Since its inception in 2006, WikiLeaks has been an equal opportunity releaser of government secrets, allowing the world to see the subterfuge and double dealings by presidents, prime ministers and government officials from countries all over the world, actions that have led to the perpetuation of war, corruption, scandal, assassinations, suppression of truth, and other ministrations that are manifestations of a closed system.

WikiLeaks has even been credited with helping to spark the Arab Spring of 2011, because of the diplomatic cables they leaked that revealed the level of corruption in Tunisia. It was this leaking of information that directly led to the overthrow of the presidency in Tunisia, which then had direct bearing on other Middle Eastern countries that were ruled by despots. The uprising in the Middle East then spread to the United States, where it manifested in the Occupy Movement of fall 2011.

An individual who is an open system is someone who is open to new ideas, and allows these new ideas to foster their own growth and evolution. Someone with an open system approach to life combines their analytic thinking capacities with their intuitive feeling capacities, so that they will not be locked into a mode of thinking in which they are ruled solely by rational thinking, devoid of feeling. We truly have infinite capacity to learn and grow—to do so, we need to think with both head and heart.

If you are a closed system thinker, then you tend to be more rigid in thought, and have trouble with the ability to intuit. You won't trust your feelings, or if you do, you'll go with knee-jerk gut instincts that aren't always well-thought out.

In order to come up with solutions to problems, be they of a personal, relationship, professional, or political nature, an open system, whether individual or organization, knows that, in the words of the physicist Richard Feynman, "If we want to solve a problem that we have never solved before, we must leave the door to the unknown ajar."

A closed system is like a feedback loop that goes around and around in circles, with no ability to get outside itself. An open system, like Feynman says, always leaves an opening, a door ajar, in order for the solution to come forth.

At the core of a Quantum Revolution is an open systems approach, in individuals—people committed to truth, transparency, openness, new solutions, the unknown, peace, harmony and love (these are all the hallmarks of an open system, and an open future)—and in organizations. Organizations are groupings of people, so they are only as strong as the people who comprise them.

8. Getting Past Greed and Selfishness

"Greed is a bottomless pit which exhausts the person in an endless effort to satisfy the need without ever reaching satisfaction."— Erich Fromm

"If we go on the way we have, the fault is our greed and if we are not willing to change, we will disappear from the face of the globe, to be replaced by the insect." — Jacques Yves Cousteau

"Earth provides enough to satisfy every man's need, but not every man's greed" — Mohandas Gandhi

It comes down to this: there comes a time when enough is enough. How much do any of us need? What do we do with all that we accumulate? If we are blessed with abundance and prosperity, do we share it with others or keep it for ourselves? Is it everyman for themselves, or is there a sense that we are all in this together? What is the innate temperament of people: selfishness or unselfishness?

"Greed is good," is the famous line uttered

by Gordon Gekko, from the Oliver Stone directed film, *Wall Street*. The film, which came out in 1987, epitomized the times, when corporate raiders like the fictional Gekko (who was modeled after a number of corporate raiders) initiated hostile takeovers of companies that enriched people like Gekko at the expense of the company and the workers of the company being taken over.

Interestingly enough, the film, while attempting to point out the insidious nature of greed and what people will do to gain money, power and influence, was instead influential in inspiring people to work on Wall Street. The principals of the film, Charlie Sheen, Michael Douglas and Oliver Stone, all commented how over the years people would still approach them and say that they became stockbrokers because of their respective characters in the film.

Speaking of Wall Street, the financial industry has had a cyclic history of collapses over its history, with the most recent one in 2008 only the latest to rear its ugly head—this one almost took down the economic systems of the U.S. and Europe. Each financial collapse has gone the same way: government regulations that were in place to oversee the financial industry are eased, or loopholes in the regulations that are big enough to drive a truck through are figured out, and in the process, the financial industry runs amok with an untethered glee towards the yellow brick road of unfettered profits. There are numerous people in the financial industry who have figured out the rules of the game and have mastered a way around those rules, and by so doing, have made millions and billions of dollars. Sadly, when the game is discovered, they at most receive a slap on the wrist, even though their naked greed ends up causing pain and suffering to millions and millions of people worldwide.

Greed and selfishness is rooted in fear, of not having enough. This fear emanates from our reptilian brain, the R-brain, and our base animal nature, one that dictates instincts of survival. These instincts warn us to get ours before someone takes it from us, because there is not enough to go around.

Greed is also the hallmark of closed thinking. With closed thinking, the perception is that there are finite limits to everything, with scarcity being seen as always looming in the consciousness. You have to get yours—for yourself and your tribe—otherwise someone else, or another tribe, will take it. You learn to see the world as us versus them, which creates physical and mental boundaries between people. You will do whatever it takes to keep what you have and to get more, whether that means having to steal, lie or kill to achieve your ends.

When a person is ruled by greed and selfishness, one of their mantras is "the ends justify the means." This phrase, originating from Niccolo Machiavelli's book *"The Prince,"* is interpreted to mean doing anything whatsoever that is required to get the result you want, regardless of the methods used. It does not matter whether these methods are legal or illegal, fair or foul, kind or cruel, truth or lies, democratic or dictatorial, or good or evil.

To steer away from the greed mentality—and in the process become more giving, selfless and considerate of how your actions impact others—means adopting a more open way of thinking. One easy way to do so is to adopt the concept known as "generalized reciprocity" or "generalized exchange"; or as it's also popularly known, "pay it forward."

The concept underlying pay it forward dates back to the year 317 BC and the comedic play *"Dyskolos,"* also known as *"The Misanthrope,"* by the Ancient Greek playwright Menander.

The play tells the story of a young, rich man, Sostratos, who falls in love with a young peasant woman. After finally convincing the woman's father to allow him to marry her, the young man goes to see his own father, Kallippides, to convince him also to be allowed to marry his love.

Kallippides balks at the thought of taking a pauper into the family. Sostratos scolds his father, pointing out that wealth is inherently unstable, "and everything you have is not yours but luck's." Therefore, the son explains, Kallippides should not bedgrudge sharing wealth with others; money can't be held forever, and luck will simply assign that wealth to someone else someday, perhaps to someone less deserving.

The son argues that wealth imposes upon its owner a responsibility to act nobly, and to "make rich as many people as you can by your own efforts. For this act never dies."

Sostratos tells his father that what goes around comes around: By acting nobly now, Kallippides may himself—in a future moment of need—benefit from someone else's kindness. Sostratos finally persuades Kallippides that it is far better to have "a visible friend than invisible wealth which you keep buried away."

The concept of pay it forward was described by Benjamin Franklin, in a letter to Benjamin Webb dated April 25, 1784:

> I do not pretend to give such a Sum; I only lend it to you. When you meet with another honest Man in similar Distress, you must pay me by lending this Sum to him; enjoining him to discharge the Debt by a like operation, when he shall be able, and shall meet with another opportunity. I hope it may thus go thro' many hands, before it meets with a Knave that will stop its Progress. This is a trick of mine for doing a deal of good with a little money.

The term "pay it forward" was popularized by Robert A. Heinlein in his book *Between Planets*, published in 1951:

> The banker reached into the folds of his gown, pulled out a single credit note. "But eat first—a full belly steadies the judgment. Do me the honor of accepting this as our welcome to the newcomer." His pride said no; his stomach said YES! Don took it and

said, "Uh, thanks! That's awfully kind of you. I'll pay it back, first chance." "Instead, pay it forward to some other brother who needs it."

Heinlein both preached and practiced this philosophy: now the Heinlein Society, a humanitarian organization founded in his name, does so.

The concept also appears in the novel *Dandelion Wine* by Ray Bradbury, published in 1957, when the main character Douglas Spaulding is reflecting on his life being saved by Mr. Jonas, the Junkman:

> How do I thank Mr. Jonas, he wondered, for what he's done? How do I thank him, how pay him back? No way, no way at all. You just can't pay. What then? What? Pass it on somehow, he thought, pass it on to someone else. Keep the chain moving. Look around, find someone, and pass it on. That was the only way....

The 1999 novel *Pay It Forward,* written by Catherine Ryan Hyde, ushered the concept into the mainstream and was further brought into the public consciousness with the 2000 film adaptation of the same name.

In the book and movie, pay it forward is described as an obligation to do three good deeds for others in repayment of a good deed that one receives. Such good deeds should be things that the other person cannot accomplish on their own. In this way, the need to help one another can spread exponentially through society, creating a social movement with the goal of making the world a better place.

Paying it forward is altruism at its finest, and is also known as practicing random acts of kindness. It is a way that opens your heart and mind —making you an open thinker—just by a simple act, a constant choice to do good. It also allows you to transcend acts of greed and selfishness by elevating you to a more noble and civilized way of being and doing.

9. Wall Street is a Mirror of All of Us

"You can out-distance that which is running after you, but not what is running inside you."
— Rwandan Proverb

"Money it's a hit
Don't give me that do goody good bullshit
I'm in the hi-fidelity first class traveling set
And I think I need a Lear jet" — *Pink Floyd*

"I have met the enemy and he is us." — *Pogo*

There is nothing wrong with making money. There is nothing wrong with making a lot of money, although if you are on that path, the key is not to let blind ambition in the pursuit of money change you and your basic core values. When that occurs, greed steps in and becomes an overpowering force in your life.

I think it's safe to say that we all admire people who have made a lot of money and have contributed useful things to society that promote the public good. When Steve Jobs died in October 2011, there was a huge outpouring of love for him, and he was deified, because of what he and the companies he started—Apple Computer and Pixar Animation Studios—did.

Other wealthy people, alive or dead, who have earned the public's respect for the way they have made their wealth and/or their convictions and principles include Richard Branson, Bill Gates, Warren Buffet, Paul Newman, George Soros and Ted Turner.

The slogan "We are the 99%" designed by the Occupy Wall Street movement was aimed at drawing a line between the haves and have-nots. Most of the 1%'s who are the object of scorn are those connected with Wall Street: those who dealt in risky derivatives, mortgage schemes, and other Ponzi permutations that helped tank the global economy. These people, unfettered by government regulation (they successfully lobbied to weaken government oversight) and ripe with greed, acted in the same manner and with the same motivations as the last breed of bankers who helped destroy the global economy, during the Great Depression.

Yet, there are some 1%'s, some connected with Wall Street and some who are not, who acknowledge and understand that there is a great divide in the U.S.

Billionaire hedge fund manager Jim Chanos

is one of them; he has gone public with his objection to tax policies weighted toward the 1%, saying "I have a problem with private capital asking for lower tax rates on certain forms of income that I believe are income, not returns on capital, than say teachers, soldiers, fireman and policeman."

Chanos also believes 1%'s who can't see why Americans are angry are seriously out of touch. "They say we live in an 'aspirational society,' but many of those in the 1% accuse others of class warfare and bemoan the fact that the president dubs them millionaires and billionaires. Well, I'm pretty sure most of the 99% would still aspire to be called the same thing!"

Philadelphia lawyer and philanthropist Dan Berger, a member of the Patriotic Millionaires for Fiscal Strength, has been hitting the airwaves and writing for quite awhile explaining why current tax policy unfairly favors the rich—and why that's dangerous for everyone. Berger is concerned about the dysfunction created by the concentration of wealth at the top, and worries that we have unlearned the lessons of the Great Depression—the last time such concentration devastated the country. "We are in a golden age of the cult of wealth," he warns. "Economic, social, and political life by, of, and for the 1% is an old story in the history of world civilization—one which inevitably ends badly."

Over the last decade, incomes for the richest 1% of Americans grew faster than that of any other group. CEO pay has soared 300 percent since 1990, while that of the average worker has risen a paltry 4 percent. If 1%'s can't be convinced that such disparities are morally wrong, Berger suggests they conjure up some "enlightened self-interest" in order to grasp what might happen if society becomes further unbalanced. He believed that the Occupy Wall Street movement was the mere "tip of the iceberg."

In 2009, Ralph Nader wrote a novel, "Only the Super-Rich Can Save Us," in which he proposed that a group of 17 billionaires, motivated by enlightened self-interest, banded together to save the U.S. and world. As Nader saw it:

> What if a cadre of superrich individuals tried to become a driving force in America to organize and institutionalize the interests of the citizens of this troubled nation? What if some of America's most powerful individuals decided it was time to fix our government and return the power to the

people? What if a national political party were formed with the sole purpose of advancing clean elections? What if these seventeen superrich individuals decided to galvanize a movement for alternative forms of energy that will effectively clean up the environment? What if together they took on corporate goliaths and Congress to provide the necessities of life and advance the solutions so long left on the shelf by an avaricious oligarchy? What could happen?

Nader's book laid out a fictional premise for how billionaires would be our saviors. But remember: it's a work of fiction. There's only one way to save us, to get us out of the place we're in. It's up to each one of us, because we're all in this together.

We're all human beings, first and foremost, whether you are a 99%'er or a 1%'er. We all have the same strengths, weakness, foibles and flaws. We are all ruled by the lesser emotions and instincts, such as fear, greed and selfishness, and the higher emotions and instincts, such as love, altruism and enlightenment.

It's not us versus them. Wall Street is a

reflection of all of us. It's actually wrong to create a divide in which it is said on one side are the 99%'ers and on the other side are the 1%'ers. We are all in this together—we are the 100%.

Greed emanates from the shadow aspect of ourselves, from the blind spot, the part we don't see. When we run away from ourselves, we move towards the dark side and the baser human emotions. When we move closer to ourselves, and live closer to our truth, we move towards the light and the highest human emotions.

There are people in the 99% bracket who are engulfed by greed, just as there are people in the 1% bracket who try to live closer to the light: where your station in life is doesn't by itself make you a good or bad person, although it is safe to say that the crimes committed by those in the 1% category have the ability to do more harm and hurt more people than the crimes committed by those in the 99% category. As Woody Guthrie sang in his song "Pretty Boy Floyd":

> Yes, as through this world I've wandered
> I've seen lots of funny men;
> Some will rob you with a six-gun,
> And some with a fountain pen.

> And as through your life you travel,
> Yes, as through your life you roam,
> You won't never see an outlaw
> Drive a family from their home.

There have been many revolutions throughout the course of history. Generally, the revolutions that have occurred have thrown out the despotic and corrupt ruling class—the 1%'ers—and replaced them with the proletariats—the 99%.

But most of these revolutions end up failing, because when the 99%'ers take power, they succumb to the same level of greed, corrupted by absolute power and influence. As the Beatles sang in *"Revolution":* "When you want money for people with minds that hate, All I can tell you is brother you have to wait."

To have a successful revolution—one that doesn't just shuffle the deck and replace the faces but not the underlying thinking and soul mechanisms that created the problems—takes a movement towards self-awareness, self-realization and enlightened thinking: a Quantum Revolution.

10. Personal/Quantum Transformation = Global Transformation

"Personal transformation can and does have global effects. As we go, so goes the world, for the world is us. The revolution that will save the world is ultimately a personal one." — Marianne Williamson

"Be the change that you wish to see in the world."
— *Mohandas Gandhi*

"Don't ask what the world needs. Ask what makes you come alive, and go do it. Because what the world needs is people who have come alive."
— *Howard Thurman*

For a Quantum Revolution to affect profound change and transformation in the world means for profound change and transformation to occur in individuals—as we go, so goes the world. Deep-rooted personal transformation is intricately connected with deep-rooted global transformation.

Our societal and global problems are systemic—the issues are so entrenched that to fix things will take rethinking and reimagining how we conduct ourselves in the world. We need to shift our consciousness and evolve our thinking to higher levels of perception in order to meet the challenges ahead.

It's not enough to change systems by external measures alone, by shuffling the deck. We need internal measures also, the ability to look at ourselves and know ourselves better, in order to change ourselves. Systems, large or small, whether they are governments, global corporations, or organic food coops, are made of individuals—and change begins with an individual's input.

All change begins from within, just as the roots of creating world peace begin with creating individual peace. If you want to be the change that you wish to see in the world, as Gandhi said, you have to be willing to see yourself honestly and truthfully, and be aware of who you are. To become a more aware person, you have to develop self-awareness and self-realization. You have to know who you are.

Societal transformation and inciting a Quantum Revolution is no easy task, but neither is personal/quantum transformation. Each is the opposite side of the same coin. Societal transformation entails looking outside yourself in order to build a more peaceful and sustainable world. Personal/quantum transformation entails looking within to build a more peaceful and sustainable you.

The more transformed you are, the more evolved you are, and the more evolved you are, the more you become a complete and integrated human being.

A complete and integrated human being is someone who is physically, emotionally and spiritually attuned to themselves, and has a wise and sophisticated understanding of themselves and the world. They are a holistic thinker, and see the visible and invisible interconnections that thread us all together.

Personal transformation means being intellectually and emotionally honest with yourself and to know yourself as best as possible. We all have blind spots, but someone who has attained a modicum of personal transformation, when brought face-to-face with their blind spot, will not run away from it and instead will allow it to shine the light of awareness on the aspects of their personality and consciousness that they had been numb to.

It takes courage to do so, and it can be

painful to be confronted by your ego and the stories it makes up to sustain you in a world of its own making, but if you can go past it, you can become truly liberated—as is said, the truth will set you free.

When you become more liberated, you become more fully formed as a person. You start shedding the baggage that has held you down, and you become lighter of mind, body and soul, and less dense. Your thinking becomes clearer, and habits, thoughts and actions that were part of your routine, patterns from your past that were permanently etched into the forefront of your consciousness so as to create who you are in the present, start to be shed, so that you can become a new person, the person of the future.

Embedded in the caterpillar is what are known as imaginal cells, cellular imaginings of what the caterpillar is to become. It lives its life with the essence of this idea in its consciousness. At first the caterpillar fights it, and attempts to destroy these cells, because the cells are so totally different from normal caterpillar cells that its immune system sees these cells as the enemy.

But as imaginal cells are destroyed, more and more new ones crop up in its place, until the caterpillar's immune system can't destroy them all. And then the imaginal cells, which contain the story of the butterfly, start to work together, passing information into the caterpillar's consciousness that it is to become something new.

As these new cells start to synchronize and resonate in tandem, the caterpillar realizes what it needs to do. It forms a chrysalis, and starts to break itself down into a kind of liquid. It creates a biological chaos, and from this chaos transformation takes place until a new order is created—the butterfly.

The butterfly, born anew from the imaginal cells of the caterpillar, goes through a complete transformation in order to finds it way in the world, having shed its old skin in order to become something new, created not by the patterns of the past, but by the hopes and wishes of the future.

This is what occurs when we go through personal/quantum transformation. No longer are we bound by patterns of the past, because we have shed the skin of the old habitual ways—instead we are propelled by the hopes and wishes of the future. We all have imaginal cells in us, caterpillars and humans alike, beckoning us towards a brighter way. I believe the imaginal cells in us glimmer with the twinkling of what a more positive, holistic and sustainable world looks like—this is the dream. Each of us carries the hope and potential for a brighter future, individually and collectively. It's just a matter of shedding the baggage, shedding the skin, and not destroying the imaginal cells within because they threaten us.

To nurture the imaginal cells and allow them to flourish begins with finding your inner stillness and center of being. Blaise Pascal, the 17th century French scientist and philosopher said, "All of humanity's problems stem from man's inability to sit quietly in a room alone." Be still, be quiet, give yourself to moments of contemplation, and find your sense of inner peace. Then you will hear the whispers of the new and be on the path of continuous growth and evolution, taking you in directions you never thought possible.

As you follow this path, your metamorphosis will transpire, and you will be transformed. As the transformation ensues, you will realize that you are part of the web of life, a web that tells us that as one person creates a ripple in the web, the entire matrix begins to reverberate.

The theory of the 100th monkey states that as enough people change, the change becomes rooted in the fabric of society. Thus, as each of us becomes transformed, society's orientation will become transformed. Even though the change will be resisted, because imaginal cells are seen as foreign objects to be destroyed, they will continue to grow and flourish, until the ideal they represent blossoms and proliferates.

At the same time, it's not enough to sit back and think, all I have to do is work on myself to change the world. This is true on the one hand, yet at the same time, you always have to consider your place in the whole, and think what can I do to change things, be it big or small.

11. Becoming a More Complete Human Being

"If you want to be a leader, you have to be a real human being. You must recognize the true meaning of life before you can become a great leader. You must understand yourself first." — Confucius

"Becoming an effective, exemplary leader is the same as becoming a fully integrated human being." — Warren Bennis

"To heal a person, one must first be a person." — Rabbi Abraham Heschel, in an address to the American Medical Association

What does it mean to be a more complete human being? We are rich and complex creatures, greater than the sum of our parts. We have a physical presence, a cognitive presence, an emotional presence, an intellectual presence, and a spiritual presence. All of these comprise who we are.

The developmental psychologist Howard Gardner explains it a different way, stating that we have multiple intelligences, or various and distinctive ways in which the mind works and perceive things. These are linguistic, logic-mathematical, musical, spatial, bodily/kinesthetic, interpersonal, intrapersonal, and naturalistic. None of us are dominant in every one of these intelligences, but we are strong in more than one of these.

In other words, we are multifaceted, and impossible to pigeonhole, as we are composed of many aspects. It is safe to say that we all are square pegs trying to fit into round holes.

To be a more complete human, you have to be fully integrated with all these segments of yourself, and be more congruent and authentic with whom you truly are. You have to have a certain transcendence, in that you have to be all these fragments, yet be greater than all.

It takes a certain degree of self-discovery and self-awareness to be fully integrated, because you have to know yourself, be comfortable with yourself, and be more evolved in your thinking. It also takes a certain degree of courage—you have to be willing to look at yourself and your blind spots and be ready to acknowledge your flaws and foibles and try and improve on them.

Completeness is encoded in the imaginal

cells, which means that being complete is embedded in our DNA, and once the imaginal cells flourish, so does our completeness. Yet it's easy to cover up this genetic code by being caught up in the story of who you are, as opposed to who you truly are.

When we get caught up in our story—which is the ego's attempt to override our truth by replacing it with its own myth—we lose congruency. To recover our congruency and authenticity, we need to strip away the junk and pierce through the layers.

When your mind continually chatters with its incessant streams of thought, that's when you get caught up in the ego's myth. And when you quiet the stream and quiet the mind, that's when you are able to find the gaps in the incessant streams of thought, and achieve congruency.

It's not about attaining perfection—none of us are perfect, and we don't want to become such perfectionists that we strive for an ideal that may not be attainable. At the same time, we all have room to improve, once we become self-aware and realize the ego's myth and the chinks in our armor that hold us back from realizing our greater potential.

We are also meant to live a healthy life, a

more fulfilled life, a conscious life, and a more awakened life—and this too is what it means to be a more complete and integrated human being.

An integrated human being is more emotionally mature, wise, far-thinking, far-reaching, conscientious, compassionate, passionate, joyful, soulful, empathetic, humble, highly intelligent (though not necessarily book smart), and intuitive.

When you are more integrated, you recognize patterns and bring together connections. You have vision, and you think long-term. You become a natural leader, because people gravitate to you. People want to be near an integrated person, as it inspires them to open up their cocoons and liberate their imaginal cells.

As more people become self-aware and complete human beings, greater numbers of leaders will help steer us forward, with their vision acting as their guide. Yet at the same time, we are all leaders and have this capability, so you don't have to sit and wait for someone to lead you along—you are a leader in your own right.

When you become a more complete human being, you become a person. That is why Rabbi Abraham Heschel, in his address to the AMA said,

"To heal a person, once must first be a person."

In regards to healing, I'd like to say a few words about it, since I work in the field of medicine and healing and wrote a previous book, *"Quantum-Integral Medicine: Towards a New Science of Healing and Human Potential,"* about the nature of healing.

Healing is not something anyone does to you—healing is something that comes from the inside out. Each one of us has an innate healing system capable of healing, if given the opportunity and the proper tools. A health provider can play a crucial role in the healing process, if they are a complete human being, a person. Their presence can inspire the imaginal cells within the patient, ones that have a remembrance of what true health is, to blossom and spring forth.

Healing is not a magical process. It emanates out of resonance, where healer and patient forge a union. The healer may be a physician, or they may be an acupuncturist, herbalist, chiropractor, energy worker, psychologist, naturopath, homeopath, shaman, or a practitioner of another modality. The healer's maturity as a person will show itself in their kindness, compassion, integrity, wisdom, transparency, authenticity and generosity, and this can then inspire the patient to heal. And as a person heals, they will become whole, and with it, more congruent and more integrated.

Just as a health provider who is a fully complete human being can help a patient become healthier and more integrated, so can a leader who is a more fully complete human being help society transform itself into a more sustainable and positive world. As Ralph Waldo Emerson said, "Our chief want is someone who will inspire us to be what we know we could be."

Part Two:
The Keys to a
Quantum Revolution

In this section, I highlight what I feel are the different keys to creating a Quantum Revolution. The first three chapters are on Personal/Quantum Transformation—the ability to be the change you wish to see in the world. The subsequent chapters in this section discuss the keys to creating that change in the world, by using our full powers and capabilities.

A. Personal/Quantum Transformation

12. Low Density Lifestyle

"There is more to life than increasing its speed."
— Mohandas Gandhi

"Half our life is spent trying to find something to do with the time we have rushed through life trying to save." — Will Rogers

"For fast-acting relief, try slowing down." — Lily Tomlin

Life moves extremely fast these days, and most of us struggle just to keep pace. Technology has created many wondrous things, yet it's easy to stay so wired that the moments of silence and peace become fewer and fewer. How can you find your center and balance point, and hear your inner voice and intuition, when the external noise is so loud? And how can you know what your heart wants, and what your deepest needs are, when they are drowned out by the ceaseless media drone that tells you how you should be thinking and what your needs should be?

This is important, because in this age of the 24/7 news cycle; advertisements blaring at us to buy the latest and greatest (and convincing people that their self-worth is equated by having the latest and greatest); gadgets galore; and a pop culture that, always trying to find the balance between art and commerce, has slanted heavily towards the sometimes crassness of commerce and forgotten the beauty of art; it is easy to forget that there is an entire world that exists outside of the clamor.

This is the world of deeper meaning, the world of inner richness, the world of nature, art, beauty, love, and peace, and knowing who you are and what matters most. How can we dream of a beautiful, peaceful, engaging and sustainable life for ourselves and the world, when we can't find the time, place or space to hear the lyrical sound of silence and nothingness?

When we live this way, we can more readily embrace that which is important, authentic and has meaning, and reject that which is superficial, meaningless and serves no one. This is possible because in the silence you can come closer to hearing your own truth, and also touch upon a higher truth—the collective dream of humanity to live in a more integrated and sustainable way.

That is not to say that you have to quit your job, throw away your TV and gadgets, and move to an ashram. If you are so inclined, feel free to do so. But what the world needs now, more so than ever before, is people who are of this world and who carry within them a degree of wisdom, and have an ability to hear and listen to their own inner longings and what their heart is telling them. These are people who live by a principled truth that is fluid rather than dogmatic and absolutist, and the chatter and noise of the popular media and culture do not influence them or affect their thinking.

Henry David Thoreau said, "If a man loses pace with his companions, perhaps it is because he hears a different drummer. Let him step to the music which he hears, however measured, or far away." Going to the beat of a different drummer means being far from the madding crowd, and forging your own path. As you do so, you will be capable of opening your eyes and seeing things as they truly should be, not as they are presently constituted.

A Low Density Lifestyle is a good phrase to capture this way of living and being. It is a way oriented towards living in a more balanced and less stressed way, and in a calm, clear and focused manner, on an everyday basis. When living this way, with the help of regular practices such as meditation and mindfulness; quiet and stillness;

eating a plant-based, whole-foods oriented diet; movement; being in nature; and tending to your emotional well-being; you feel lighter, less heavy and less dense, and you feel like everything is flowing and that you're clicking on all cylinders. In other words, you are utilizing more of your potential, and because of it, you think and act in a more integrated way.

Sadly, the vast majority do not live in such a manner. Between of our fast-paced lifestyle and a feeling of being overwhelmed, people are burning the candle at both ends and living with an inordinate amount of stress. The end result is unhealthy and unsustainable lifestyles. And when you are living in this kind of way, who has the time or inclination to see beyond yourself, when you are basically treading water to keep up the pace?

When you are living in this manner, it is easier to accept the status quo, and give your power over to others and become apathetic, because life is too busy and too demanding to live in any other fashion. You don't want to make waves and you don't want to step out of the box and away from the norm, because there is safety and security in what you are doing, even if it's not working. Most people will choose the known entity, even if it isn't sustainable, rather than taking a chance with the unknown, because choosing the unknown will take them far from their comfort zone.

People living this type of fast-paced lifestyle usually don't feel well. It may start with a feeling of low energy and being easily upset and irritable, and from there continue onto depression, anxiety and a feeling of being lost. From a standpoint of the physical symptoms that are characteristic, some of the most common ones are obesity, diabetes, high blood pressure, high cholesterol and coronary artery disease.

And living this way doesn't discriminate between the 1%'ers and 99%'ers. People of all ages and backgrounds are living this fast-paced, high-stress lifestyle—it doesn't matter what your race, color, creed, sexual orientation, or size of your bank account is. In fact, people with bigger bank accounts sometimes think that more money buys better medical care, and that's all they need to become healthier. But as we know, better medical care just means more drugs and more surgeries and procedures. That has nothing to do with real health or getting off the merry-go-round of an unsustainable lifestyle.

The healthier your lifestyle and the more of

a Low Density Lifestyle you live, the more alive and passionate will you feel, and the more will you be committed to a meaningful life that makes a difference, and to not accepting the unsustainable aspects of the status quo.

The visionaries of this world, past and present, were innovators, pioneers who made a difference in various realms, including the arts, technology, politics, philosophy, spirituality, the law, medicine, and science. These were people who were willing to take a chance and step into the unknown, and veer away from their own personal comfort zone, because of something within that pushed them forward. They listened to their heart, and paid attention to their own inner dialogue. These are the role models for all of us.

13. Healing and Release

"Healing may not be so much about getting better, as about letting go of everything that isn't you—all of the expectations, all of the beliefs—and becoming who you are." — Rachel Naomi Remen

"People have a hard time letting go of their suffering. Out of a fear of the unknown, they prefer suffering that is familiar." — Thich Nhat Hanh

"Some of us think holding on makes us strong; but sometimes it is letting go." — Herman Hesse

The health of its citizens is a direct reflection and byproduct of the economic, political, cultural, sociological and spiritual health of a nation. In that regard, the United States is a sick country, and one that knows nothing about what healing truly is.

Its medical system is highly flawed, in danger of collapse and is primarily a sick-care system. The U.S. spends twice as much on health care per capita than any other country, yet people are twice as sick due to the high rates of chronic disease: 75% of all health care dollars are spent on patients with one or more chronic conditions, many of which can be prevented, including diabetes, obesity, heart disease, lung disease, high blood pressure, and cancer. Meanwhile, life expectancy at birth in the U.S. is an average of 78.14 years, which ranks 47th in highest total life expectancy compared to other countries.

On top of all that, the U.S. is the only developed nation in the world without a true universal health care system. No wonder that about half of the bankruptcy filings are due to medical expenses.

And then there's drugs: pharmaceutical sales in the U.S. are a $300 billion a year industry, with over 3.5 billion prescriptions a year written. The best-selling class of drugs are the statins, used for lowering cholesterol; the second-best selling class of drugs are those for acid reflux; and the third best-selling class of drugs sold are anti-depressants. As a consequence of all the drugs taken by Americans, medication side effects are the fourth leading cause of death.

The cost of drugs has skyrocketed, and insurance companies pass on these costs to the consumer by raising premiums. From 2000 to 2006, overall inflation increased 3.5%, wages increased 3.8%, while health care premiums increased 87%.

To change the health care system of the U.S., it will take a philosophical shift in understanding what healing is all about. The medical system's mission is to help people be healthy, yet the modern medical system knows nothing about delivering health.

And because of that, the United States, the richest and most prosperous nation on the earth, is one of the unhealthiest countries on the planet. When a person is unhealthy, it is hard for them to see beyond their physical, emotional and spiritual ailments to vision a greater world to live in. Instead, because of their ailments, they are stuck in a quagmire in which they live in a disempowered and apathetic way.

For anyone who has gotten onto the path of health and wellness and recovered their health, you know what it feels like to experience vitality—you feel energized, passionate and fulfilled, and you attain a heightened state of mental clarity. These feelings should be basic human rights, as they are not that hard to attain. But when you are not conditioned to think and act in this way, when this is not the direction that a society is programmed to aim for, when there are vested corporate interests in keeping you unhealthy, you do not follow that road.

As I stated in the very first chapter, an integral part of our dilemma is the fact that we are disconnected from ourselves, causing us to live in a fragmented way. We do not think in a holistic manner: we are divorced from nature, divorced from our intuition, and divorced from listening to what our body and mind tell us. How can we vision a more sustainable and positive world if we can't think and live in an integrated way? Fragmented thinking and living will only lead to fragmented solutions.

And without health, without knowing what healing is, the mind and body will continue to be fragmented. One of the things healing does is allow you to become more integrated.

Diet plays an important role in healing in many ways. Not only does eating a plant-based, whole-foods oriented diet help you to feel better and think more clearly and more holistically, but it helps you become more in touch with where your food comes from. One of the by-products of the modern American diet is the fact that people are so far removed and disconnected from where their food comes from that they don't even think about its origin; because of this, the great majority of Americans are not eating real foods anymore.

Instead, they're eating what the author Michael Pollan calls "edible food-like substances."

Not too long ago, all foods were real foods, and primarily whole foods. Now, much of the diet are concoctions of quasi-foods. When people eat a steady diet of this, how can they be expected to be healthy or to think clearly? To paraphrase Karl Marx, it could be said that edible food-like substances are the opiate of the masses.

Eating a healthier diet is the ground zero of healing, and now more than ever before, the information for what constitutes a healthy diet is part of pop culture, which has allowed this knowledge to become ingrained in the public consciousness.

Yet, so many people cannot and will not change their eating habits to healthier ones. That is because the choice of the foods we desire, and our attachments to food, are psychological in nature, and deep-rooted at that.

These psychological attachments to food drill down to the roots of healing: healing is not just physical, although eating a healthy diet, which is a physical approach to healing, is integral to health. Healing, at its core, is psychospiritual—it's a process of clearing out and releasing: releasing old memories, wounds, traumas, dogmas, emotions, and other baggage that impedes our ability to be a fully integrated human being.

Why do people make poor choices with their diet, and make other lifestyle choices that impact their health in a negative way, even if they know what they are doing can cause harm to themselves? It is because of deeply held belief systems that are so ingrained that they are beyond the scope of the cognitive mind—they are in the blind spot.

Cognitive talk therapy is important to the healing process, but it has its limitations, because it is just the ego's perceptions. Beyond cognitive thought lies an entire realm of deep, inner space, an inner infinity, a nonverbal realm filled with thought forms, energies, and essences. These are where the patterns that we hold onto are tenaciously bound up, living outside of the mind's eye.

In Chinese medicine, chronic diseases are known as knotty diseases. They are seen as a deeply embedded intangible, energetic knot within the body, created by years of lifestyle choices, behavioral patterns, attitudes, insults, and other factors that can play a detrimental role. To treat the knotty diseases, true healing needs to take place, a healing process that is multidimensional in scope, and takes into account the physical, emotional and spiritual.

People who have the knotty diseases generally have holding patterns in their mind and body, and these patterns often manifest as chronic pain. These holding patterns and the chronic pain it causes tend to occupy a lot of mental bandwidth and end up taking on a life of its own. It will consume your energy and cause you to obsess over it, feeding on negativity and reinforcing behavior and lifestyle patterns that will keep feeding it, in order to have dominion over you.

When you are in this state, it is near impossible to see beyond yourself and your own problems. Why would you care about trying to create a more positive, holistic and sustainable society and world, when that seems so far away and abstract, compared to your own real world problems?

It seems that the U.S. and all its problems of unsustainability—caused primarily by short-sighted greed and the dominance of short-term gain over the common good—requires an unhealthy populace so caught up in their own ills and ailments that they don't have the energy, attention or concern to question the validity of letting the status quo continue as is. For if a population was healthier, and living in a more integrated way and thinking in a more holistic way, the questioning of the status quo might better ensue, and with it the cultivation and emergence of creative solutions that can move us forward.

It's not that there's an intentional conspiracy being carried out to keep people living in an unhealthy way in order to maintain the status quo. No, it's just a byproduct of the way things are done, and the collateral damage from the cost of doing business. This is what happens when you have a society that doesn't put a value on wisdom and enlightened thinking in formulating public policy and how business should conduct itself. The disconnect that is going on has its own momentum and has taken on its own life cycle.

Actually, you could say that this is what happens when people who are byproducts of our unhealthy system—and due to it have their own physical and mental holding patterns—gain positions of power, whether in politics or as captains of industry.

This disconnected, fragmented and nonintegrated way of living, of holding patterns locked into the body and mind, can only be healed through a psychospiritual approach, one that helps a person become whole again. This is a process in which things need to be released, not suppressed, in order to help a person's energy flow easier.

The process is not hard, but it takes a commitment to seeing it through because it means opening up to the blind spots, and releasing the holding patterns. A plant-based, whole-foods diet is important, as are gentle, body-mind integrated approaches that encourage and cultivate openness.

The more we find our way onto the healing path, the greater will our desire be to join in with the collective dream of creating a more sustainable world, and then finding our way to it.

Watch: an Interview with Donna Eden and David Feinstein, co-authors of the book *Energy Medicine*, from the video interview series, "Interviews with the Leading Edge." http://drmichaelwayne.com/leadingedge/donna-eden-david-feinstein/

14. Self-Mastery

"Knowing others is intelligence; knowing yourself is true wisdom. Mastering others is strength; mastering yourself is true power." — Lao-tzu

"The true value of the human being is determined by the measure and the sense in which one has attained liberation from the self." — Albert Einstein

"The difference between great people and everyone else is that great people create their lives actively, while everyone else is created by their lives, passively waiting to see where life takes them next. The difference between the two is the difference between living fully and just existing." — Michael E. Gerber

The most important life skill you can learn in this lifetime is to take ownership and responsibility for your own actions and deeds, and not blame anyone else for what you do. Even when you are faced with circumstances outside your own control, there is always a part of the situation that is under your own control—nobody can make you do something you don't want to do.

The late comedian Flip Wilson created a number of raucous and ribald characters, but his most famous persona, Geraldine, stood out from the crowd. Geraldine was an uncontrollable shopaholic, and in one of the skits Geraldine came home with a new and expensive dress, upsetting her preacher husband, who bemoaned the cost of it. Geraldine told him, as a way to shirk responsibility, "The devil made me do it. The devil made me buy this dress."

There is no devil, there is no person who makes you buy anything. The only person who makes you buy anything is yourself. This is the core teaching of 12-step programs, that you must take ownership of what you do—no one makes you drink, take drugs, shop, or any other addictive behaviors. Only you do it, and only you can undo it—with support if need be, as none of us are in it alone.

When we embody this premise, when we take ownership of who we are and live our lives actively and not passively, we are then on the path towards self-mastery—we don't wait for things to happen to us and instead we make them happen.

Yet, there is so much conditioning and habitual behavior patterns that push us away from this principle. In the desire to fit in, to run with the pack and not act or think different, we end up conforming and not thinking for ourselves, and go along with what we are told and accept the norm for what it is.

It takes courage to step outside what is expected of you, because you are up against not just the expectations of society, community, friends, family, intimate partners, and others, but against your own deeply held and ingrained belief and behavior patterns.

Where do these patterns that are so tightly enmeshed in your body, mind and soul originate from? They arise from your family of origin, creating a family structure that embeds itself in your mind and psyche and also creates your persona. It's an indoctrination that doesn't allow you to act from your authenticity, but instead from the grip of the family structure and the expectations that come with it.

In most family structures, the parents take from the child what they need to exist and cope. It's not done out of hate or vindictiveness, it's just the way your parents felt about themselves. Families are the most unenlightened aspect of our society, and it creates a lot of deep-rooted, subconscious thought patterns that then drive your life and hold you back from taking ownership, because you are acting out of drives that you aren't even aware of.

Family structures have rules, codes and expectations, some spoken and most unspoken, and these rules, codes and expectations are designed as mechanisms to follow. They shape and disempower you, rather than empower you. In the family structure, intimacy and co-dependency intermingle, creating a complicated internal programming that is hard to unravel, both as a child and adult.

This family structure creates who you are as an adult, and bounds you by the language of that structure. Additionally, in the family structure there is one person who is the most influential in your life, and it is that person that is the one whose energy you carry throughout your adult life.

And so, the family structure and the story it creates lies at the heart of who we are and our inability to take ownership and responsibility for the actions we take. How can we be in mastery of ourselves when we don't know where the behaviors and thought patterns are coming from?

Self-mastery means moving beyond the family structure, and doing it from love. It doesn't mean burning bridges and cutting off ties with your family structure; instead you skillfully move beyond in a way predicated on actions aimed towards transcendence and enlightenment. It takes courage to do this, because in doing this you are acting from a more evolved segment of your mind that is willing to transcend your personal self-created comfort zone and take you to points unknown. And to do so means you have to understand the root of your behavioral patterns and then let go of them—you have to be aware of when you get triggered and activated and where that is coming from.

    The rules and regulations we create as adults are from the family structure, and are created out of a feeling of not being safe. This is why it takes courage to move towards self-mastery and beyond the family structure, because when you become aware of your deeply ingrained patterns and start saying no to them, it can feel scary as you step away from the familiar and towards the unknown.

    It's a journey to break out of the mold: this is the journey of enlightenment. It is a journey of self-discovery, of understanding better who you are and what has created your modus operandi. It allows you to come into your own power, as you approach a more powerful version of yourself. You no longer have to distort yourself to fit into a mold of the expectations of others; now you can create your own mold, personally tailored to fit around your own authenticity.

If we don't understand and transcend our family structure, then the people who come into our lives—our friends, associates, business partners, significant others, and others—will lead us to relive and repeat over and over again our own family structure and the behavior patterns they created in us.

The greed and avarice of those who are destroying the world, and their blindness to how their actions are hurting everyone, are a direct manifestation of their own family structure, of growing up unloved, manipulated and full of distortions about themselves. We need and desire these people to be healed, to be made aware of and to become enlightened about their behavior patterns.

Yet the same can be said of all us—none of us are immune to this. As I said in an earlier chapter, we are the 100%: we all are part of the human experience and all of us have the potential to go through a journey of self-discovery and find our way towards self-mastery. Each one of us needs to be on the path that allows us to see beyond the blind spot in our body and mind, and to understand the family structure and take ownership of how it affects us. Therein lies the foundation for self-mastery and enlightenment, and with it, the path to creating a personal and quantum transformation not only in yourself but in the world.

B. Societal Transformation

15. Vision and Leadership

"The visionary starts with a clean sheet of paper, and re-imagines the world." — *Malcolm Gladwell*

"If you want to build a ship, don't herd people together to collect wood and don't assign them tasks and work, but rather teach them to long for the endless immensity of the sea." — *Antoine de Saint-Exupery*

"If your actions inspire others to dream more, learn more, do more and become more, you are a leader." — *John Quincy Adams*

In the fall of 2011, when the Occupy movement was front and center in the news, one of the critiques of the Occupy movement was that there were no leaders, that it was an amorphous organization with no central structure; or that perhaps they were following Bob Dylan's edict from *"Subterranean Homesick Blues,"* when he says "Don't follow leaders, watch the parking meters."

What the Occupy movement was striving for was getting away from the standard version of top down, hierarchical organizations, where a person at the top, a President or CEO, announces his dictates, and the organization follows suit.

If we subscribe to the fact that we are all natural born leaders and that we all have visionary capabilities, then a top down organization isn't necessary—instead an alternative model can be designed. This type of organization can be run in a collaborative manner or there may be one person who steers the organization. If it is one person, this is because this person has earned the right to do so based on their clear-headed and farsighted vision, with a track record that has proven that.

A top down hierarchical organization has the potential to disempower and disengage all those who sit below the top of the pyramid, while an organization run on a collaborative basis, or by one person based on their vision, has the potential to engage and empower all those who are involved with it.

That's not to say all top down, hierarchical organizations are bad, and all collaborative organizations are good, because there are some hierarchical organizations run by leaders who are visionaries and fully integrated humans, while there are some collaborative organizations and organizations run by one individual that are dysfunctional and myopic.

A collaborative has greater potential to empower people, because more people are involved in the leadership process, but that doesn't make it the perfect model. It really comes down to the organization's mission, the culture ingrained within the organization, and the person or people steering it. True leadership is based on vision and the ability to take the long view.

The problem is, most corporations are not primed to take the long view, and instead only think of the short-term, which to a corporation is defined as "how can we make the most amount of money in the shortest amount of time?"

Richard Ferry, former president and co-founder of the recruiting firm of Korn/Ferry International, spoke to the problem of this two decades ago and his observations are just as relevant today:

> Corporate America may talk, on an intellectual level, about what it'll take to succeed in the twenty-first century, but when it gets right down to decision making, all that matters is the next quarterly earnings

> report. That's what's driving much of the
> system. With that mind-set, everything
> else becomes secondary to the ability to
> deliver the next quarterly earnings push-up.
> We're on a treadmill. The reward system in
> this country is geared to the short term.

And Joseph Campbell, speaking on the same subject once said, "in medieval times, as you approached the city, your eye was taken by the cathedral. Today it's the towers of commerce. It's business, business, business, and in an escalating fashion it has gotten more short-term oriented.... You know, they're not funding the real iconoclasts today, not funding the innovators, because that's risky—that's long-term investment."

Short-term thinking is based on patterns of predictability and of being able to control variables and know outcomes. It uses analytical models that forecast what might happen in the short-term, based on patterns of the past that hopefully will repeat themselves. But analytical models don't work for long-range thinking and planning, because there are too many unpredictable factors that arise over time, too many variables beyond control.

Quantum physics and the new sciences—

chaos and complexity theories—have shown that life is turbulent and complex and not linear and sequential, in which one thing logically leads to another in an analytical cause and effect relationship. Instead, life is spontaneous, contrary, unexpected, and ambiguous. Things do not happen according to plan, and they are not reducible to tidy models.

Short-term thinking persists in grasping at neat, simple answers, when instead we should be questioning everything. It is short-term thinking that rules not just corporations but most structures in our society. Politics, of course, is a prime example, as it is rare for a long-term solution to take precedence over a short-term, quick fix.

The seed for sustainable living in the U.S. began in the 1970's, when Jimmy Carter was president. He installed solar panels on the roof of the White House, and promoted renewable resources. But short-term thinking quickly neutered his ideas, and sustainable living and renewable resources lost traction in the mainstream for several more decades.

Jimmy Carter was a visionary, as is anyone who can see into the future for the solutions. The difference between then and now is that now there are more visionaries, more people thinking long-term and coming up with solutions that can propel us into the future.

A visionary realizes that the answers are already out there, and that it is just a matter of gaining glimpses into these solutions in order to understand them. These glimpses may at first be seeds of an idea, just a kernel of truth. But the more they are developed, the more they can come to fruition.

One of the beauties of open thinking and open systems is that it allows more people to collaborate on these visionary models. As one visionary sees the glimmer and attempts to crystallize it, others can then start to collaborate on the model, and bring it to light.

The future is waiting to be born, and true visionaries and leaders are ready to embrace it. Because they are not solely bound by short-term thinking predicated on analytical, cause and effect models in which the best predictor of the present is the past, they can see that the best predictor of the present is often times the future.

The conundrum is that long-term thinking is a threat to the core of our beings, because it disrupts the myth and illusion that creates the cocoon we live in, that this is a safe, predictable world. Instead, long-term thinking represents turbulence, unpredictability and chaos. And that is why, as Joseph Campbell said, the iconoclasts and visionaries have a hard time getting funding, which means that the iconoclasts and visionaries have a hard time bringing their ideas into the public consciousness and public arena.

But it is the iconoclasts, the visionary leaders, who have the potential to change the world, and who have made the world a better place. They may be artists, entrepreneurs, politicians, athletes, spiritual teachers, inventors, scientists, musicians, writers: whatever and whoever they are, they are the ones who inspire us to do better.

Steve Jobs was one of these people, and when he died in October 2011, the emulation was in line with the inspiration he gave to others. In an interview in 1996, he said:

> When you grow up you tend to get told the world is the way it is and your life is just to live your life inside the world. Try not to bash into the walls too much. Try to have a nice family life, have fun, save a little money. That's a very limited life. Life can

be much broader once you discover one simple fact, and that is—everything around you that you call life, was made up by people that were no smarter than you. And you can change it, you can influence it, you can build your own things that other people can use. The minute that you understand that you can poke life and actually something will, you know if you push in, something will pop out the other side, that you can change it, you can mold it. That's maybe the most important thing. It's to shake off this erroneous notion that life is there and you're just gonna live in it, versus embrace it, change it, improve it, make your mark upon it. I think that's very important and however you learn that, once you learn it, you'll want to change life and make it better, cause it's kind of messed up, in a lot of ways. Once you learn that, you'll never be the same again.

One of Jobs' most brilliant ad campaigns for Apple Computer was his "Think Different" series of TV commercials. In them, he brought the iconoclast and visionary to the forefront, and made them out to be the hero—which they truly are. Here's the words to the ad:

> Here's to the crazy ones,
> the misfits,
> the rebels,
> the troublemakers.
> The round pegs in the square holes.
> The ones who see things differently.
>
> They're not fond of rules
> and they have no respect for the status quo.
>
> You can quote them,
> disagree with them,
> glorify or vilify them.
> About the only thing you can't do
> is ignore them,
> because they change things.
> They push the human race forward.
>
> And while some may see them as the crazy ones,
> we see genius.
>
> Because the people who are crazy enough to

think they can change the world
are the ones who do.

Think Different.

We all have the capacity to be visionary leaders, because we all have the capacity to think different. As more and more people do so, and envision a more positive and sustainable world and put those ideas into action, the more likely is it that we will see a Quantum Revolution happen in the coming years.

16. Quantum Consciousness

"The most important thing going forward is to break the boundaries between people so we can operate as a single intelligence. Bell's theorem implies that this is the natural state of the human world, separation without separateness. The task is to find ways to break these boundaries, so we can be in our natural state." — David Bohm

"The universe seems more like a great thought than a great machine" — Sir James Jeans

"A radical inner transformation and rise to a new level of consciousness might be the only real hope we have in the current global crisis brought on by the dominance of the Western mechanistic paradigm." — Stanislav Grof

Ingrained in every cell of our body, down to the minutest level, is the capacity to be a visionary, to be a broad holistic thinker who can peer into the future and glimpse and intuit far-ranging solutions. This is a scientific and physiological reality—it is the fabric on which our imaginal cells are created.

Traditional spiritual wisdom, especially from the East, has understood this for millennia. Thanks to understandings in the sciences, especially quantum physics, we in the West are now able to comprehend the reality of this.

What we now know is that before matter there is consciousness, and that consciousness is the ground of all being. We do not live in a mechanistic universe, run by predictable determinism—we live in a living, breathing, interconnected universe full of information, energy and uncertainty.

Sir James Jeans, a Nobel Prize winning physicist for discoveries he made in quantum physics, put it best when he said, "The universe seems more like a great thought than a great machine."

The irony of quantum physics is that to understand the implications of quantum physics requires the same broadening of mind that quantum physics says is our natural inclination. There is much to a quantum universe that is hard to comprehend and wrap the mind around, but what it insinuates is that we, individually and collectively, have great capacities to affect the world.

Granted, in new age parlance, quantum physics tends to be misappropriated, and suggests that we can create and attract anything we want just by thinking about it. It goes deeper than that, because if it were that easy we could all meditate our way to a more perfect life and world. That's not to say we shouldn't focus on the positive, because we do have a tendency to attract the type of energy we put out, but still, it's an incomplete truth to think that we can just visualize our way to a better world.

We are capable of visualizing answers though, or at least glimpses of answers, by using our inherent capacity to think in the broadest way possible. Quantum consciousness tells us that this is an infinite universe, and that we have the capacity to think infinitely, to go beyond ourselves to see new ways of doing things.

There are many critics, skeptics and naysayers who will tell you why you can't do something, or that your idea is crazy, or that you are out of step with the mainstream point of view. Yet as Robert F. Kennedy said, "There are those that look at things the way they are, and ask *why?* I dream of things that never were, and ask *why not?*"

This is a world designed by dreamers. The findings of quantum physics and quantum consciousness may be new, but the innate ability to see in the largest way possible has been an inarguable truth since the beginning of time.

The Zen tradition calls this Big Mind, and understands that the process of utilizing Big Mind signifies going beyond the dualistic voices in our head—the countless voices distorting our perception of reality that keep us entangled in our story. These voices play the role of critic, judge, vulnerable and wounded child, victim, skeptic, fixer, the controller, and numerous others.

Instead, to realize Big Mind, we need to align with the transcendent voice within, the voice that unifies our perceptions, allows us to see clearly, and allows us to feel totally awake, present and in the moment. To be in this state takes a certain degree of enlightenment, yet ironically it is such an innate part of our existence that it actually takes no effort to achieve. All it takes is waking to this reality: it's effortless, but we are so caught up in efforting that it's always moving away from us—every time we take a step closer, it moves away.

Meditation, being in stillness, and being quiet and empty are all-important steps to realizing your true nature of quantum consciousness and Big Mind. But it is no guarantee, because if it becomes effort, the target just keeps moving.

We live in a society that strives, pushes,

efforts and spins its wheels constantly. Life has a deeper meaning and there is a depth and profundity to the rhythms of the world, but if we continually strive we cannot hear or discern it. To be aligned with quantum consciousness and Big Mind is to cultivate a deep knowing of how things are.

Deep knowing entails trusting the unfolding process that life is. You may not have the answers, because you can't always know things right away—the answers often come when we are ready to hear and understand their meaning, if we are willing to trust the process.

Since the beginning of time, and throughout the millennia that humans have walked the earth, life has always been an evolutionary process, continually unfolding in new and different ways. None of us can truly predict what is down the road for any of us—we can only state probabilities, not actualities.

The butterfly effect tells us that all it takes is a ripple here or there for things to change, sometimes dramatically. It sounds scary to be confronted by such incertitude, and because of that, most of us cling to whatever stability we can find. Granted, we all crave stability—none of us can live amidst the uncertainty of chaos all the time, yet if we allow the fear of loss of control to color our choices, we start grabbing for our share before others can get it.

Without a commitment to deep knowing and an alignment with quantum consciousness and Big Mind, life becomes a roller coaster ride, leading to a feeling of helplessness in the face of everything that can happen. One way people choose to protect themselves if they live in this way is to try and control whatever they can, and try and amass all that they can.

The path our society and world is on at this point in time goes against the grain of the character of the universe, because it eschews deep knowing for simple answers that cater to fulfilling the base survival needs, such as control and stability, whether they serve the public good or not. By not aligning with quantum consciousness and Big Mind, we put ourselves at peril, because we cannot continue to sustain ourselves in the wake of the problems that we currently face.

17. Creative Intelligence

"Imagination is more important than knowledge. Knowledge is limited; imagination encircles the world" — *Albert Einstein*

"If we want to solve a problem that we have never solved before, we must leave the door to the unknown ajar." — *Richard P. Feynman*

"Everyone is born a genius, but the process of living de-geniuses them." — *Buckminster Fuller*

We are all geniuses; it is innate in each and everyone of us, and unique to each and everyone of us. Yet, as Buckminster Fuller states, the process of living de-geniuses us.

There are many pressures that cause de-geniusing—one of the main ones is conforming to the norm. As Jonathan Swift once said, "When a true genius appears in this world, you may know him by this sign, that the dunces are all in confederacy against him." To utilize your genius potential, you have to be willing to run in the opposite direction of the pack. If you're willing to do so, there is no limit to what is possible.

What holds people back from accessing their innate genius potential? The answer to this question is another question: why do we think the way we do? The answer is that we live by memes. A meme is an idea, behavior or style that spreads from person to person within a culture. A meme acts as a unit for carrying cultural ideas, symbols or practices, which can be transmitted from one mind to another through writing, speech, gestures, rituals or other imitable phenomena.

The word meme was coined by the British evolutionary biologist Richard Dawkins in his book *The Selfish Gene*, as a concept for discussion of evolutionary principles in explaining the spread of ideas and cultural phenomena. Examples of memes given in the book include melodies, catch-phrases, fashion and the technology of building arches. Malcolm Gladwell wrote, "A meme is an idea that behaves like a virus—that moves through a population, taking hold in each person it infects."

Memes can also be considered mental models, deeply held images of how the world works. Mental models impact the way people perceive the world and how they think, and often become dogmas. Mental models are subconscious drivers of actions, behaviors and thinking patterns

—people will often act out of irrational and dogmatic habits, because of their mental models.

The greatest mental model that our society lives by is that we live in a world of linear deterministic logic, or reductionism—that this is a clockwork, mechanical and predictable universe, dictated by black and white rules, where everything is either good or bad, with no shades of grey. This way of thinking deals in absolutes, seeing a world in which you are either with or against us.

This way of thinking found a critique in the climax of the film *Star Wars Episode III: Revenge of the Sith*, when Darth Vader says to Obi-Wan Kenobi, "If you're not with me, then you're my enemy," to which Obi-Wan responds, "Only a Sith deals in absolutes."

And during the U.S. war in Iraq, Stephen Colbert parodied this mentality on several occasions, such as by saying, "Either you are for the war [in Iraq] or you hate America."

By thinking in this way, and living by this meme and mental model, you give your power away to experts, because they are always assuring that life is ok and predictable and they have all the answers. By doing so, it causes you not to believe in or trust your own powers.

This is a logical universe; make no mistake about it. It's just that the type of logical universe we reside in is not based on a linear deterministic logic, but instead a creative logic predicated on discontinuities.

The roots of logical thinking go back to Aristotle, and his dictum that: A is A; What is A cannot be not-A; and Everything is either A or not-A. To Aristotle and the ancient Greeks, logic was a subset of logos, which is the power that brings the world into order. To modern thinkers, that power, logos, is logic and reason. Yet to Aristotle, that power, logos, was the active creative principle. The physicist David Bohm said creativity was a fundamental principle of the cosmos and what needed to be explained were the processes that were not creative.

The active creative principle, which both Aristotle and David Bohm understood was the power that brings the world into order, is known in modern scientific terms as discontinuities. Discontinuities are creative movements, and movements of creative emergence, because they are unknown and unpredictable.

Discontinuities are also quantum leaps, which is the way matter moves when it is born out of the infinity of the conscious, living universe. The universe moves discontinuously, as do all waves and particles—electrons come and go in their orbits, disappearing and appearing from one orbit to the next.

Creative intelligence, which is a talent innate to all of us, is the ability to go beyond your normative and ingrained thinking capabilities. It is born from the world of discontinuities and quantum leaps, from a logic that belongs to a higher order. With the use of creative intelligence you can make quantum leaps in thinking and change your memes and mental models.

There's a saying: "If you always think the way you've always thought, you'll always get what you've always got." If you're caught up in linear deterministic logic, you'll always think the same old way and become a prisoner of your thoughts, and never find a way out of any problem or crisis you get in. You will be in a continuous negative feedback loop, continually recycling similar thought patterns and reinforcing limiting habits and behaviors that don't serve you at all.

To get out of the feedback loop requires the mind to make a leap in thinking, to experience a discontinuity in thought, similar to the quantum leap an electron makes.

The discontinuity is an aha moment, when the mind opens up to the infinite nature of the universe, and we align with quantum consciousness.

Most people are stuck in the loop and aren't capable of overcoming the issues that dog them in life. They think the reason they can't do so is because of psychological impediments such as: poor self-esteem; lack of confidence; lack of encouragement; past traumas; and others. Yet, the answer to getting unstuck from the loop lies in using creative intelligence and making a leap outside the system, and in the process, taking a step beyond the memes and mental models that rule them. By utilizing our creative intelligence, we can realize more of our human potential, regardless of the psychological hurdles we face.

Creative intelligence is the creative impulse of the universe, and the creative impulse of emergence. It allows you to tap into your innate genius potential, and allows you to open your mind to quantum consciousness and Big Mind. It also allows you to take quantum leaps in thinking and consciously evolve who you are, and in the process, expand your vision and leadership capability and become a true Quantum Revolutionary.

Creative intelligence is a powerful tool for finding new ways of doing things, and for creating a positive, holistic and sustainable world. And what happens as more and more people cultivate their creative and innate genius potential? It creates a *scenius*.

Scenius is a term developed by the musician Brian Eno—it's like genius, only embedded in a scene rather than in genes. Brian Eno suggested the word to convey the extreme creativity that groups, places or scenes can occasionally generate. His actual definition is: "Scenius stands for the intelligence and the intuition of a whole cultural scene, and is the intelligence of a whole operation or group of people. It is the communal form of the concept of the genius."

Individuals immersed in a productive scenius will blossom and produce their best work. When buoyed by scenius, you act like genius. Your like-minded peers, and the entire environment, inspire you. Scenius can erupt almost anywhere, and at different scales: in a corner of a company, in a neighborhood, or in an entire region, society, or even the entire world.

The history of art and science is crammed with episodes of scenius. In modern literature there was the Algonquin Round Table, the Bloomsbury Group, the Inklings in Oxford, UK. In art and culture there was Paris in the 20s, the lofts in Soho, NYC, the folk music scene of Greenwich Village, and most recently, Burning Man. In science there was the Lunar Society in England, Building 20 at MIT, and the ever-spreading Silicon Valley.

A scenius emerges out of vibrant, cutting edge scenes or cultural niches where a group of people, often crossing disciplines and areas of expertise, are pushing into something new and rewarding each other for taking risks and challenging the status quo.

Scenius plays an important role in culture change, and historically has arisen in many different locations at points of epochal shift. In earlier times, scenius occurred in specific regions, either through direct collaboration or through the spread of ideas, or the seeds of ideas.

With the advent of the Internet and the connectivity and open culture that it offers, we have the potential for a broad-scale scenius, spurred on by the surge in creativity that Internet media is driving. Now, the potential for a world-wide scenius is relevant, and with it, the cultivation of a great leap forward in the application and forward thrust of creative intelligence.

Ideas of an open system nature will thrive in this environment, incapable of being held back from the forces of suppression used against it. The intangible power of scenius and connectivity will rise above the tangible force of repression and closed systems.

The advent and blossoming of creative intelligence and scenius on a large scale bodes well for the future, giving hope for what can emerge in the coming years.

18. Conscious Evolution

"In conscious evolution our spiritual experience expands to include resonance with the design of evolution. Our spiritual growth awakens our social potential, pressing us deeper inward to pick up that design and outward to express our creativity in the world through vocation. We work from within toward higher consciousness, greater freedom, and more complex order to effect a change in the world." — Barbara Marx Hubbard

"Evolution and revolution are part of our nature. Many believe we are passing through such a momentous transformation, a major turning point, a history-making sea change. A new and entirely different pattern of thought is beginning to emerge worldwide and in various fields of human activity." — Don Beck

"Everything is making its difference to the whole. No one is ever outside the God-Process. But it goes only where we go with it. It doesn't force us, we are the movers from the inside. It won't go forward unless we move it forward. That is why we are all so important. We cannot wait for the world to turn, for

the times to change that we may change with them, for the revolution to come and carry us round in its new course. No more will the evolutionary forces of nature propel us in their groping way through the next critical point into a new state of being. From now on, if we are to have any future, we must create that future ourselves. We ourselves are the future and we are the revolution." — Beatrice Bruteau

With the development and cultivation of vision and leadership, quantum consciousness and creative intelligence, we have the potential to see the blossoming of a new society. Conscious evolution is the tool to bring it to proper fruition.

We live in an evolving universe, and humankind is part of that evolving story. From the origins of the universe, our planet arose. From the gaseous nature of beginning earth, life forms arose. And from life forms, over the course of billions of years, humans have evolved. We have evolved on many levels from our earliest ancestors: biologically, cognitively, intellectually, culturally and spiritually. And we continue to evolve, to higher levels of awareness and higher levels of consciousness—to higher levels of being and doing.

The understanding of conscious evolution is a fairly new concept. It explains that we have developed enough self-awareness to have become aware of the process of evolution itself, and because of this we can choose to be in alignment with the evolutionary process and work towards cultivating higher levels of being and doing. This represents a monumental shift in our ability to perceive and affect the shape of things to come.

We now stand on the brink of a revolution that will change the course of human development. For the first time in the three and a half million-year history of human intelligence, that very intelligence has realized that it can understand, analyze, and nurture itself. By applying itself to itself it can develop new ways of thinking that are far more flexible and powerful than the traditional modes of thought currently in use throughout the world.

Consciousness has been evolving for billions of years. We are becoming aware that through our own consciousness the universe can know itself. This awareness reveals incredible new potential for our individual and collective humanity. We now realize that we are affecting our own evolution by everything we do.

Evolution is not random, nor is it intelligent design—there are a lot of unintelligent things in the universe. Evolution is an impulse, a desire to be more and do more—it is coded into our being.

Plato, Aristotle and the ancient Greeks pondered the question of evolution and understood that the universe had a greater purpose, what they called a teleology. They believed that the purpose of all beings was to fulfill their inherent potential.

Modern philosophers have looked at the teleological perspective and have realized that evolution goes through general stages that are universally shared. It is also understood that although the evolutionary drive is one towards greater awareness, greater meaning, and greater consciousness, the universe is also a meandering one, and that we are just as capable of blowing ourselves up as we are of developing heightened powers of awareness, vision, and creative intelligence.

Conscious evolution instructs us that we are capable of evolving to these higher capabilities, but does not tell us that this is a guarantee. We are the first species on this Earth aware that we can destroy ourselves by our own action. This may be the greatest wake-up call to the evolution of consciousness of and by itself.

The 20th and 21st centuries have seen rapid and dramatic changes on many scales, from the development of new sciences and technologies, to more profound spiritual understandings. We are attaining new levels of evolution—as our cognitive knowledge evolves, we are codifying the quantum sciences and the new sciences of complexity and emergence and developing new technologies. And as our spiritual knowledge evolves, we are becoming wiser.

Furthermore, conscious evolution shows us that the course of evolution has a certain developmental arc to it, a pathway of memes that has been mapped out by leading edge thinkers in various fields.

It has been seen that human behavior goes through universal stages of being, with each successive level allowing for a more mature, wise, and enlightened level of thinking. At the lesser levels, thinking tends to be clouded by self-absorption, fear and the baser survival needs; at higher levels, thinking tends to be holistic, integrated, interdisciplinary, visionary, and more focused on the greater good.

Crises are often evolutionary drivers. When

faced with a difficult path ahead, nature will usually find a new and creative solution to a problem. In that same way, our ability to consciously evolve has become a necessity, because of the problems that we are facing and the need to come up with new and creative solutions that don't comprise the same old way of doing things.

At this juncture in human history, urgent global crises challenge us to learn to live sustainably, harmoniously, in collaboration, and with gratitude towards one another and with the living universe. The changes required of humanity are broad, deep, and far reaching. Only by acting swiftly and creatively can we birth a planetary culture that will bring well-being to every form of life in the Earth community.

We are being called, each and every one of us, to move to the forefront, to consciously evolve, and to become leaders. When you do so, you will feel something course through your veins. That is because intense ambition, success and leadership—the burning drive to do more and be more, to bring your vision to fruition, to make a mark—evolve out of complex, real world dynamics. It is predicated on being in alignment with the force of consciousness, with the evolutionary impulse of the universe, so that you experience vocational arousal and become aligned with your purpose. It then becomes part of you, part of your psyche, so that you're ready to give it everything you've got.

And as you give yourself to conscious evolution and the creative impulse of the universe, you become aware of a future waiting to emerge, and see yourself as an instrument to midwife this emerging future. This vision—to create one of the greatest social and cultural transformations in history—and its potential to create a peaceful, just, holistic, compassionate, positive, and sustainable society, has been the dream of individuals and societies for millennia.

In the past, the tools, technology and know-how to shepherd in such a transformation was just a glimmer of a dream, an imaginal cell beyond the adjacent possible of the times. But now, we have the understanding to bring it within our grasp and see it crystallize in front of our eyes.

Watch: an Interview with Barbara Marx Hubbard, Founder, Foundation for Conscious Evolution, from the video interview series, "Interviews with the Leading Edge." http://drmichaelwayne.com/leadingedge/barbara-marx-hubbard/

19. Presencing and Emergence

"We have no idea of our capacity to create the world anew." — Peter Senge

"Out beyond ideas of right doing and wrong doing, there is a Field. I will meet you there." — Rumi

"When leaders develop the capacity to come near to the source, they experience the future as if it is wanting to be born." — Otto Scharmer

Presencing is a term, developed by the social scientist Otto Scharmer, that brings together the words "pre-sensing" and "presence." It means to pre-sense and bring into presence one's highest future potential. Every human being and social system has the potential to activate this deeper capacity. Presencing can connect us more deeply both to what wants to emerge in the world and to our emerging, higher Self.

Emergence is a concept from complexity theory, and it shows how complex systems and patterns evolve and arise out of a multiplicity of relatively simple interactions; it is a creative process that is the key property of all living and open systems on earth. Emergence is the movement to higher levels of order and sophistication in order to adapt to the environment and the variables presented. At times, emergence arises out of chaos: the chaos of a personal life, relationships, a social system, a culture, a society, or the world.

Taken together, when you enter into the realm of presencing, you become aware of a future seeking to emerge, which implies that the future has intentionality. It is also about bringing into presence and into the present your highest potential, your highest future possibility as a human being, and the highest potential for society and the world.

Presencing also implies a deep knowing, knowing what is right, and what is true. Your highest future possibility is related to your own highest purpose or intention. Exploring your future potential is intimately connected with your evolving, authentic Self. This evolving future field can be experienced as a being that is looking at you.

As we work with the evolving future field, we start to use ourselves as an instrument for something better to emerge, which can help us become open to our larger purpose. Everyone is born with a destiny or purpose—the journey is to find it.

The core of presencing is waking up together—waking up to who we really are by linking with and acting from our highest future Self—and by using the Self as a vehicle for bringing forth new worlds. And presencing and emergence together leads to action shaped by the field of the future rather than by the patterns of the past.

At the center of our being is pure essence. When we go beyond ego, when we see ourselves for who we truly are, we are connected to Source and situated in a realm of deep knowing. This is when we are in contact with answers still unseen and still unknown.

There is much to our universe that we do not know, and much of it is beyond comprehension, or at least beyond articulating what exactly it is that is out there. Only four percent of our universe is matter; the other 96 percent is dark matter and dark energy. Dark matter, which makes up 23 percent of the universe, is defined as wispy subatomic particles, while dark energy, which makes up 73 percent of the universe, is an energy that is causing the universe to expand at an ever-increasing rate. Scientists may call it dark energy, but in reality they have no idea what it is.

And since we are a microcosm of the macrocosm, it is quite possible that this is our biochemical and biophysical makeup, that only a small fraction of who we are is solid matter and the rest is an amorphous amalgam of energetic and information-rich space.

The point of this is that at the core of the universe, and ourselves, is a cloud of unknowing. This is the Source, the inner and outer infinity that we touch when we enter the sphere of presencing and deep knowing.

When we try to know and predict outcomes and try to control things down to the last detail, we become locked into analytical time, when the past is the greatest predictor of the present. But when we let go and surrender to the deep knowing, then something greater than us occurs, and we discover that the field of the future has bearing on the present.

We live not in a full three-dimensional world of physics, but instead a multi-dimensional world of psychophysics, where time, space, mind, body, laws of physics, future, present and past all interact in a fashion different than what we have come to expect. That is not to say that you can travel through time and go back to a different era. At this point in time, that is not physically possible and defies the known laws of physics. But what is possible is that the mind can connect to a greater reality, to the 96 percent of the universe that is not matter, and go beyond time and space to touch onto the field of the future, and with it, to feel, sense, see, touch, taste and intuit what the future can bring.

When we go beyond ego to essence, we can get a glimpse of the field of the future, even if it's just a shadow or a kernel of light of this field. We need to let go of our preconceptions, and the ego's desires and strivings, and hold in our hearts an agenda that doesn't push solely our own individual needs, but instead the highest collective dream of humanity.

We know that the highest collective dream of humanity has always been a world of sustainability and peace, even if we don't fully know how it will come. But as more people experience presencing and emergence—and realize their visionary and leadership capabilities, access their quantum consciousness, utilize their creative and innate genius potential, consciously evolve, master their self, and apply their innate healing capabilities to themselves and gently release that which they are holding onto—they will more readily touch the Source and enter the realm of deep knowing, and in that instance, they will start to see the answers and solutions, and begin to bring them to reality.

Part 3: Viva la Revolucion!

20. Understanding Happiness: Lessons From Bhutan

"A table, a chair, a bowl of fruit and a violin; what else does a man need to be happy?" — Albert Einstein

"Money never made a man happy yet, nor will it. There is nothing in its nature to produce happiness. The more a man has, the more he wants. Instead of its filling a vacuum, it makes one. If it satisfies one want, it doubles and trebles that want another way." — Benjamin Franklin

"Happiness cannot come from without. It must come from within. It is not what we see and touch or that which others do for us which makes us happy; it is that which we think and feel and do, first for the other fellow and then for ourselves." — Helen Keller

What does happiness have to do with a Quantum Revolution? Everything.

We all want to be happy and enjoy life. Yet,

how many people know what happiness is? In the United States, it seems to be a vanishing commodity. The U.S, with five percent of the world's population, consumes 65 percent of the world's psychotropic drugs, tranquilizers, and mood enhancers; currently there are over 30 million people suffering from depression in the U.S. And the World Health Organization predicts that by 2030, depression will be the number one health issue worldwide.

Most people equate happiness with attaining things—success, status, material objects. And as they strive for more and more to achieve that happiness, the only thing they find is less happiness. If you keep striving for more, it usually becomes a moving target, and you find that the more you attain, the more you want.

As I mentioned in an earlier chapter, greed is behind the desire to attain more. But the motivation for greed is often, whether consciously or unconsciously, the desire to be happy and fulfilled. And it is this drive for more that has created a society and world of unsustainable crises, because the subtext for that drive is usually to attain more at all costs, regardless of its impact on others or the environment.

The problem is that unsustainability creates unhappiness for many of the world's citizens, because of how it impacts natural resources. So while a few are trying to produce more happiness for themselves by generating more wealth, they are simultaneously creating more unhappiness for the vast majority.

This is a vicious cycle that can never end unless the true meaning of happiness is fully understood. A few years ago, former U.S. President Jimmy Carter was asked, "President Carter, have you come to any new perspectives about what matters in life, now that you're older?" His answer was to the point: "Earlier in my life I thought the things that mattered were the things that you could see, like your car, your house, your wealth, your property, your office. But as I've grown older I've become convinced that the things that matter most are the things that you can't see—the love you share with others, your inner purpose, your comfort with who you are." If more people understood what true happiness really is, it's possible that, of and by itself, could help pave the path towards a sustainable world.

Happiness is not about the material possessions you have, but about the intangibles: how you feel about who you are, the work you do, your purpose, the relationships you have, and the love you share. The important lesson to be learned is that it's the simple things in life that matter most.

If you remember the classic film *Citizen Kane*, the movie begins with the death of the millionaire Charles Kane as he utters the words "Rosebud." The film's story is told primarily through flashbacks, as a reporter attempts to find out what Rosebud signifies; at the end it turns out to be a sled from his childhood. At the end of his life, as his life flashed in front of him, Charles Kane realized that the most important thing, what gave him the most amount of joy, was his childhood sled, which to him represented the innocence of youth.

Another thing that leads to the cultivation of happiness is to give of yourself and to serve others. As the Dalai Lama said, "If you want others to be happy, practice compassion. If you want to be happy, practice compassion." Life has more meaning and purpose when we are inclusive in our thinking and care about the welfare of others. But when we pursue our own needs regardless of how it affects others, we lose purpose and meaning, along with a sense of compassion.

The World Database of Happiness presents one of the most interesting examinations into whether or not money buys happiness. This database is an ongoing register of scientific research on the subjective enjoyment of life. The scores are based on responses to a question about satisfaction with life and perceptions of personal well-being, the answers to which were rated on a numerical scale ranging from dissatisfied to satisfied. Rating scales ranged from 0 to 10.

As you can see from the following list, when you place each country's GDP per capita (in current U.S. dollars), there is not much correlation between how much money people make and how happy they feel. For example, Guatemalans have the same happiness score as Canadians, although their income is only one-eighth as much. What does tend to reliably correlate with happiness is the quality of relationships with family and friends and a personal sense of belonging to one's community.

Ranking Country Score/National GDP Per Capita

1. Denmark 8.2 $37,400
2. Colombia 8.1 $6,700
3. Switzerland 8.1 $41,100
4. Austria 8.0 $38,400
5. Iceland 7.8 $38,800
6. Australia 7.7 $36,300
7. Finland 7.7 $35,300
8. Sweden 7.7 $36,500
9. Canada 7.6 $38,400
10. Guatemala 7.6 $4,700
11. Ireland 7.6 $43,100
12. Luxembourg 7.6 $80,500
13. Mexico 7.6 $12,800
14. Norway 7.6 $53,000
15. Netherlands 7.5 $38,500
16. Malta 7.5 $22,900
17. United States 7.4 $45,800
18. Belgium 7.3 $35,300
19. El Salvador 7.2 $5,800
20. New Zealand 7.2 $26,400
21. . Germany 7.2 $34,200
22. United Kingdom 7.1 $35,100
23. Honduras 7.1 $4,100
24. Kuwait 7.0 $39,300
25. Saudi Arabia 7.0 $23,200
26. Cyprus 6.9 $27,400
27. Italy 6.9 $30,400
28. Spain 6.9 $30,100
29. Argentina 6.8 $13,300
30. Brazil 6.8 $9,700
31. Dominican Republic 6.8 $7,000
32. Singapore 6.8 $49,700
33. Venezuela 6.8 $12,200
34. Chile 6.7 $13,900
35. Israel 6.7 $25,800
36. Slovenia 6.7 $27,200

37. Uruguay 6.7 $11,600
38. Indonesia 6.6 $3,700
39. France 6.5 $33,200
40. Czech Republic 6.4 $24,200
41. Greece 6.4 $29,200
42. Nigeria 6.4 $2,000
43. Philippines 6.4 $3,400
44. China 6.3 $5,300
45. India 6.2 $2,700
46. Japan 6.2 $33,600
47. Taiwan 6.2 $30,100
48. Uzbekistan 6.2 $2,300
49. Kyrgyzstan 6.1 $2,000
50. Vietnam 6.1 $2,600
51. Iran 6.0 $10,600
52. Peru 6.0 $7,800
53. Portugal 6.0 $21,700
54. Croatia 5.9 $15,500
55. Poland 5.9 $16,300
56. Bolivia 5.8 $4,000
57. Korea, South 5.8 $24,800
58. Bangladesh 5.7 $1,300
59. Senegal 5.7 $1,700
60. Hungary 5.6 $19,000
61. Morocco 5.6 $4,100
62. Montenegro 5.5 $3,800
63. Slovakia 5.5 $20,300
64. South Africa 5.5 $9,800
65. Lebanon 5.3 $11,300
66. Algeria 5.2 $6,500
67. Jordan 5.2 $4,900
68. Kenya 5.2 $1,700
69. Turkey 5.2 $12,900
70. Bosnia/Herzegovina 5.1 $7,000
71. Estonia 5.1 $21,100
72. Serbia 5.1 $10,400
73. Uganda 5.1 $900
74. Romania 5.0 $11,400
75. Azerbaijan 4.9 $7,700
76. Macedonia 4.9 $8,500
77. Mali 4.9 $1,000
78. Egypt 4.8 $5,500
79. Ghana 4.8 $1,400
80. Iraq 4.7 $3,600
81. Latvia 4.7 $17,400

82. Lithuania 4.6 $17,700
83. Albania 4.4 $6,300
84. Angola 4.4 $5,600
85. Russia 4.4 $14,700
86. Pakistan 4.3 $2,600
87. Bulgaria 4.2 $11,300
88. Georgia 4.1 $4,700
89. Belarus 4.0 $10,900
90. Armenia 3.7 $4,900
91. Ukraine 3.6 $6,900
92. Moldova 3.5 $2,900
93. Zimbabwe 3.3 $200
94. Tanzania 3.2 $1,300

In surveys such as this, the impoverished people of Calcutta, India, living in crude shacks and with little access to clean water, register about even with Americans on the happiness scale—and well ahead of the Chinese, South Koreans, and Japanese. Meanwhile, relatively poor Guatemalans and Columbians appear to be among the happiest people on the globe.

And in looking at the survey, you can see how the U.S., one of the richest countries in the world, is ranked 17th amongst countries in terms of the happiness quotient of its citizens. It ranked behind a number of poorer countries, such as Columbia, Guatemala and Mexico, and ranked even with El Salvador and Honduras.

The World Database of Happiness found that happiness is directly correlated to economic well-being up to the level of meeting basic needs and a little beyond, but after that there's no correlation between money and happiness. Furthermore, they determined that there is a definite disconnect between happiness and growing income levels after a certain point.

Money is not bad, but it can't buy you true happiness. True happiness comes from a sense of fulfillment, of purpose, of following a dream, of feeding your soul, and of helping others. A person who is a true financial success is someone who says that what they did to achieve that success wasn't done for the money, but instead was done for the love of their project and for their service to humanity, and that the money was secondary. It is when the pursuit of money is the primary goal, at the exclusion of all other goals, that a person often loses their soul and forgets what truly matters.

One country that didn't make the World Database of Happiness list, due to a lack of data collected, is the nation of Bhutan. Articles, books and documentaries have been produced about this unique Buddhist country tucked high in the Himalayas because of its designation as "The Happiest Country on Earth."

Bhutan has received their designation

because they have made happiness part of their economic and political system, by measuring their country's success not by a GNP (Gross National Product) or GDP (Gross Domestic Product) but by a GNH—Gross National Happiness.

The concept of GNH was originated in 1972 by the fourth king of Bhutan, King Jigme Singye Wangchuck, when he was 18 years old. He used the phrase to signal his commitment to building an economy that would serve Bhutan's unique culture, based on Buddhist spiritual values. His son, Jigme Kheser Wangchuck, who in 2006 at the age of 26 became the fifth king of Bhutan when his father abdicated, has continued to evolve the concept of GNH.

Not too long ago, Bhutan was a closed society, not interested in interacting with the world, nor well developed. It was the fourth king who felt the time had come to open Bhutan up to the world and slowly modernize and adapt to the rapidly changing global economy. As he began this process, he came up with the idea of Gross National Happiness as the key to growth for his country, because he wanted to keep traditional values while embracing globalization.

The Bhutanese government, in developing Gross National Happiness, determined that beneficial development of human society takes place when material and spiritual development occur side by side to complement and reinforce each other. They put forth four pillars of GNH: good governance; balanced economic development; environmental preservation; preserving and promoting culture.

Let's look at each of these four pillars more closely:

Good Governance: Bhutan_believes that their government must be responsive to the needs of the people, free of corruption, and emphasize justice, integrity and effectiveness. In drafting their constitution with the emphasis on GNH, Bhutan looked at over 50 different constitutions to determine how they could create a better system of democracy.

Balanced Economic Development: The goal in formulating this pillar was to raise the standard of living for all citizens, for which they realized growth was required. Bhutan knew it needed to open to the ways of the modern world, but it wanted to do it in a measured way that allowed for growth and prosperity without sacrificing basic values.

Environmental Preservation: Buddhist precepts teach that all of life is sacred, so preserving the environment is imperative to Bhutan. To them, the natural world is an integral component of life and a source of sustenance and happiness, and so economic policies and the movement towards growth take sustainability into account in devising policies.

Preserving and Promoting Culture: The Bhutanese people see culture as the very basis of their lives and that which gives them their national identity. Their culture is Buddhist, one that talks about justice, helping people, equality, the sacredness of life, and that satisfaction comes from within. GNH is deeply rooted in this ethos, and from the Buddhist teachings of non-attachment and not being overly materialistic.

Interestingly, if you were to go around the country of Bhutan and ask the people what they think of Gross National Happiness, most of the people would not even know what it is, because they already live that way without knowing the details. They are happy and content because they have inner peace, which allows them to be grateful for what they have. One Bhutanese man, on being asked what was it like to live in his country, said, "It's like living in heaven."

As other organizations and governments have come to study the Bhutanese approach, they have come to understand that a country does not have to be Buddhist in order to value sustainable development, cultural integrity, ecosystem conservation, and good governance.

Working together with an international group of researchers, the Center for Bhutan Studies has further evolved the four pillars into eight general contributors to happiness: physical, mental and spiritual health; time-balance; social and community vitality; cultural vitality; education; living standards; good governance; and ecological vitality.

The international community of researchers that has collaborated with the Center for Bhutan Studies has shown that the happiness of a country's citizens is firmly intertwined with the physical, emotional and economic wellbeing of its citizens, and that the more humane and compassionate a government is, the more it takes care of all its people. This is why in Bhutan certain rights, including employment, education and health care, are guaranteed to everyone.

Bhutan is showing the world what can be done with a new, more enlightened form of progress. They saw what growth and development was doing to the world, and they saw that something was missing—namely true happiness. This is what inspired the fourth king of Bhutan, Jigme Singye Wangchuck, at the tender young age of 18, to develop the concept of Gross National Happiness.

The Bhutanese believe that any nation on earth can adapt GNH into their system of government, and by so doing, develop a country that is open, democratic and progressive. They believe that as Buddhism speaks of the middle path, there is a middle way towards happiness—one that doesn't deny the movement towards globalization and growth, but believes it can be done with the help of visionary leaders who are committed to guiding their people towards true happiness and sharing this ethos with all.

Another country that is considered to be one of the happiest countries in the world is Iceland. Iceland has gone through its own difficult times in recent years, with the nation's economy devastated by the recent global economic crisis. Iceland has been through many trials and tribulations throughout their thousand-year-old history, but one thing that has bound them together as a people is a genetic link. Everyone in Iceland is related to everyone else, so they have biologically and historically always felt connected to each other, and have looked out for one another at all times throughout the course of their history.

The simple fact is that more is not necessarily better when it comes to enjoying life and feeling satisfied. More may be more, but it is never enough. We're caught up in the myth that by achieving and going up the ladder and having more stuff, we'll feel full inside. It just isn't so. It's not about the material things you can show the world, but about how you feel about the work you do, the relationships you have, and the love you share.

That's what really matters, and that's the optimal and most enlightened way to build a society.

21. Towards an Open Future

"There is a concept which corrupts and upsets all others. I refer not to Evil, whose limited realm is that of ethics, I refer to the infinite." — Jorge Luis Borges

"The future ain't what it used to be." — Yogi Berra

"It is said that the present is pregnant with the future." — Voltaire

The era we live in is far different than any other time in history—we have the potential to take society and the world to new levels of hopeful possibility. Although there is much positive occurring in these emerging times, there is also much that can lead us to fret and worry if we will make it through. Yet, as Robert Frost once said, "the best way out is through."

We are entering a new epoch, that of an open future, and it is an open future that is the way through. We as individuals are evolving, and parallel with this, the future is evolving. It is this interplay, between an evolving future and our own evolution, that is the impetus for the transformation ahead.

In chapter 7, I talked about open and closed, how open systems succeed and closed systems fail. As I said in that chapter, an open system is where there is a degree of openness that allows for the cross-pollination and cross-fertilization of minds and ideas, which then allows ideas to take shape; while a closed system is rigid and mechanistic, and continues doing the same thing and operating in the same way, even if the approach has proven not to work. Furthermore, I mentioned that open systems are based on an infinite and expanding universe, one that continually evolves and grows, while a closed system is based on finiteness, one that does its best to resist growth and maintain the status quo, because it can't see how to get past itself.

And this is the direction we are evolving towards—an open systems future. An open future is a path that creates an evolution towards our greatest capacities: the capacity to be more open, more free, and more wise and insightful, and to become integrative, cross-disciplinary thinkers. An open future takes us towards the ideal put forth by the French paleontologist, evolutionary philosopher and

Jesuit priest Pierre Teilhard de Chardin when he said, "Remain true to yourself, but move ever upward toward greater consciousness and greater love!"

Interestingly enough, de Chardin, who lived from 1881 to 1955, was far ahead of his time when he spoke out and wrote articles and books that stated that not only was our universe evolving, but that humans were also evolving, and as the two trajectories intertwined, humans had the potential to aspire to higher capacities of consciousness and love. His ideas came up against a society and Church that was extremely closed, and for the sins of his omissions, the Church banned his writings from being published, came close to excommunicating him, and sent him packing to the far outposts of China, where they hoped he would never be heard from again.

But Pierre Teilhard de Chardin's ideas live on, and the wisdom and truth of his teachings are more transparent now, as society evolves closer to his vision. We are moving towards an open future, and as we do so, we have the possibility of achieving this movement towards greater consciousness and love.

How are we seeing de Chardin's ideas come to life, and what does it mean for the future? He saw the emergence of an open future, and with it, he understood that this was the hope for the future.

It is now upon us, in very real and practical ways. I first realized this a few years back when I was watching a documentary entitled "Revolution OS," a film ostensibly about the people who created and first shared open source software; the underlying theme of the film was the desire for people to connect and share from a place devoid of agendas and selfish desires, and for whom the desire to share knowledge and information was the highest form of service and love.

We are now seeing this approach spread through the economy in a way that is making it an unstoppable force. The chains of separation and isolation are being removed, and because of this, people are better able to move towards more connectivity and sharing by ways that were once either impossible, suppressed by artificial boundaries, or discouraged. Some of this movement is because of technology and the internet, some is spurred by profit motive, and some is predicated on the innate desire for people to be open, transparent, and sharing of knowledge, insights, and ultimately, love.

It was Kevin Kelly, the founding editor of *Wired* magazine who stated, in a 2002 article in the *Wall Street Journal*, that the "Web runs on love, not greed." He specified that only a small percentage of websites are crassly commercial, while the rest are "created and maintained out of passion, enthusiasm, a sense of civic obligation, or simply on the faith that it may later provide some economic use…" and that "millions of smaller sites and hundreds of millions of users do the heavy work of creating content that is used and linked. These will be paid entirely in the gift economy."

Kelly singlehandedly put his finger on the pulse of what was happening in society as a whole, that the economy is transforming into what he called "a gift economy," one in which people put an emphasis on finding ways to share information and ideas, with the hope, if that is their goal, that the money will follow suit at a later time. Or if money isn't the goal, that the ability to move ideas and information past the artificial boundaries that separate people is the payback—and the gift.

Openness and connectivity is what takes

down walls and barriers. In the late 1980's, Mikhail Gorbachev, the President of the U.S.S.R., instituted glasnost, or openness and transparency, as official Soviet policy. With glasnost came less censorship and greater freedom of information, and within a few years, the Soviet empire went through monumental changes—the U.S.S.R. came to an end, and with it, the Berlin Wall came crashing down and the countries that were part of the so-called Iron Curtain also became free of Soviet dominion.

To this day, many of these countries are still experiencing growing pains, as to grow from a tightly-controlled dictatorship to a democracy means having to undo decades, and even centuries, of behavior patterns and deeply-ingrained tribal customs. There is no doubt that it was Gorbachev's decision to implement glasnost, which was a phrase known in Russia since at least the end of the 18th century, that spearheaded such quick and tumultuous change.

The well-known TED (Technology, Entertainment, Design) Talks are another example of how the transition to an open future bodes well for the future. Billed as "Ideas Worth Spreading," the TED

Talks began as a one-time conference in 1984. The first conference featured demos of the Sony compact disc, and one of the first demonstrations of the Apple Macintosh computer. Presentations were given by mathematician Benoit Mandelbrot and influential members of the digerati community, like Nicholas Negroponte and Stewart Brand.

The event was not financially successful, and it wasn't until 1990 before the second conference was organized. From 1990 onward, a growing community of "TEDsters" gathered annually at the event in Monterey, California, until 2009, when it was relocated to Long Beach, California due to a substantial increase in attendees. Initially, the speakers came from the fields of expertise behind the acronym TED, but during the nineties, the roster of presenters broadened to include scientists, philosophers, musicians, religious leaders, philanthropists and many others. The programs were costly, exclusive and by invitation only—in 2006 it cost $4,400 to attend. It was a fascinating event, but it was also something that represented a closed system, as it was only open to those who had the means to attend, and were invited to do so.

In 2006, the people behind TED decided to post a handful of TED presentations online, and in January 2007 they raised the number of videos online to 44. This was such a success that they decided to raise the bar and make TED a full-fledged online event and community, and in April 2007 the newly redesigned TED website was launched with 100 videos, and with the launch, TED went full force forward into an open future. From its inception as an exclusive, invitation-only event, TED had transformed itself into an organization that anyone, in any part of the world, could easily access, free of charge.

Currently there are over 1500 talks posted, with 5-7 new ones posted each week; the total viewership for all the videos is well over one billion views. Here is what Chris Anderson, the curator of the TED Talks, had to say about the change in philosophy of TED:

> It used to be 800 people getting together once a year; now it's about a million people a day watching TEDTalks online. When we first put up a few of the talks as an experiment, we got such impassioned

responses that we decided to flip the organization on its head and think of ourselves not so much as a conference but as "ideas worth spreading," building a big website around it. The conference is still the engine, but the website is the amplifier that takes the ideas to the world.

It is in the mission statement of TED that the power of an open system comes into full view:

> We believe passionately in the power of ideas to change attitudes, lives and ultimately, the world. So we're building here a clearinghouse that offers free knowledge and inspiration from the world's most inspired thinkers, and also a community of curious souls to engage with ideas and each other.

An open future is the key to a more enlightened future, and one that can allow us to live more peacefully with one another in a very sustainable way. To change to a more open system would mean, as with all attempts at change, getting past the fear of the unknown—even though a closed system is dysfunctional and doesn't serve society well, it is what we know well, while an open system represents an unknown, a new model and way of doing things.

Furthermore, as Jorge Luis Borges says in the quote at the beginning of this chapter, *"There is a concept which corrupts and upsets all others. I refer not to Evil, whose limited realm is that of ethics, I refer to the infinite."* An open system, which is a representation of infinity, is a concept that corrupts and upsets all others.

Yet the truth is that our universe, and every living thing and collection of things in it, is an open system. We continue to evolve in ways that are not always predictable, so the unknown is a steady part of life.

The beauty of our world in the present day is that we are becoming more and more aware of this fact, and our culture, society and world are moving in that direction. And as we do so, it's best if we all get on the bus.

Creating a more open world is truly the path towards creating a better tomorrow. A more open world is predicated on your ability to be more open of mind, of thinking beyond yourself and including in your perspective the perspective of others, and also understanding how your behaviors and actions may affect others.

A closed society operates by way of a zero-sum game, in which resources are seen as finite and limited, and in order for someone to win resources, someone else has to lose them. In this scenario, if I get what I need, then you lose what you need. There are only a few winners in a zero-sum game, and many, many losers.

The survival-oriented lower part of the brain does what it can to block openness and connectivity, because in this primal segment of the brain the emphasis is on survival by any means necessary. This creates an every man for himself mentality in which the rationale for blocking connectivity is that if everyone is to be allowed access, there will be no incentive for those who want to make profits, because there will be no proprietary secrets or knowledge.

While there are times when protecting what we have and blocking connectivity may be necessary, this rationale stretches the truth at best and at worst creates an opaqueness in which truth is obscured in the name of greed and vested self-interests.

The case of Sergey Aleynikov, the only employee of Goldman Sachs to be arrested in the wake of the financial crash of 2008, is a case in point of the primal brain in action. Aleynikov actually had nothing to do with the crash; he was a top computer programmer who worked for Goldman Sachs for two years and then quit in 2009 for a more lucrative paying job with another financial firm. In the summer of 2009 he was arrested by the FBI and charged with breaking Federal law for stealing Goldman Sachs' computer code. It was Goldman Sachs who called the Feds to arrest him because they believed that the code could "manipulate markets in unfair ways."

    But it was all bogus. Aleynikov got the code through open source channels, although Goldman Sachs stamped their proprietary seal on it, to demonstrate that it was now theirs. True, once Aleynikov downloaded the code, he then set about rewriting it for Goldman Sachs' platforms, but still, it wasn't something that originated at their offices. His bigger crime was that he emailed himself the code so that he could continue to work on it, which was the nature of open source information—you took the source information, adjusted it, and then made it available for the next person.

When Aleynikov left Goldman Sachs, he did have the code, but it was useless anywhere but on Goldman Sachs' platforms. But Goldman Sachs, an organization whose main objective is the hallmark of a closed system—survival of the fittest through short-term actions that guarantee success (in other words, make unbridled profits by any means necessary)—decided to make an example of Aleynikov and have him arrested.

In December 2010 Aleynikov was convicted of two counts of theft of trade secrets and sentenced to 97 months in prison. He served almost a year in prison until his case was thrown out and he was acquitted on appeal.

It's a profound irony that for all the worldwide pain and suffering Goldman Sachs caused in 2008 and beyond—thanks to their closed system, primal-brain fueled, unbridled and unregulated aspiration to attain as much money as humanly possible—Sergey Aleynikov was the only employee of the behemoth corporation to go to jail.

An open society operates by way of a positive-sum game, in which win-win situations are the norm. If I get what I need, you also get what you need, and so everyone wins.

We are seeing an open future approach find its way to the mainstream and become more and more integrated into the prevailing economic model. Some of it is partly due to technology, yet technology is just one tool among many for creating an open future.

Just like the Berlin Wall's collapse, other walls that divide people are coming down. With the expansion and opening up of intellectual property laws, many creators of intellectual property are choosing to use the creative commons and the un-copyright as a way to openly share their work, as opposed to the traditional copyright, which only serves to create a closed wall. By opening up access, the creators of intellectual property are allowing for a sharing of materials in a way that has never occurred before in our modern age.

By allowing for the sharing of materials, it creates a pattern and thread of openness in which innovation and connectivity more readily occurs.

Ideas and innovation are more likely to blossom in environments where connection is more valued than protection, and where truth is allowed to be unrestrained. In tightly controlled environments, where the natural movement of ideas and innovation are tightly controlled, creativity is strangled.

At the heart of an open future is the power for people to connect, mind to mind and heart to heart, in ways that allow for creative expression and innovation to prosper, and an enlightened consciousness to come into existence. This movement towards an open future is an innate drive, emanating from our higher brain's evolutionary capacities and desire—as opposed to our lower-brain's survival instincts—to connect.

This drive towards connectivity grants you the ability to express yourself in ways that allow for an evolving future to unfold, and can help you aspire in the direction of the words of Pierre Teilhard de Chardin, when he said, "Remain true to yourself, but move ever upward toward greater consciousness and greater love!"

Watch: an Interview with Charles Eisenstein, author of the book, *Sacred Economics*, from the video interview series, "Interviews with the Leading Edge." http://drmichaelwayne.com/leadingedge/charles-eisenstein/

22: How to Start a Revolution

"We are now faced with the fact...that tomorrow is today. We are confronted with the fierce urgency of now...Over the bleached bones and jumbled residues of numerous civilizations are written the pathetic words—'too late.' " — *Martin Luther King, Jr.*

"If we don't change the direction, we will end up exactly where we are headed." — *Chinese proverb*

"The old economy of greed and dominion is dying. A new economy of life and partnership is struggling to be born. The outcome is ours to choose." — *David Korten*

This is my point: a new future is emerging, and we have a golden opportunity to midwife it along. Make no mistake, though: there is much volatility in the air, much to be concerned about. But the future belongs to those who see what is upon us.

An open future awaits us: this is what is emerging, blossoming and coming to fruition. It is occurring technologically, culturally, economically and spiritually—and this movement is finding its way into the mainstream. At the root of this movement towards an open future is the transformation of the individual, which is no small feat.

Walls are coming down—the walls that separate people. The Berlin Wall was an obvious example of a wall that separated people, but most of the walls are constructs of the mind. When we operate from a disconnected vantage point, and try to protect and hold onto what we believe is ours, it creates a wall that separates us from others. But those walls are no longer necessary, because we are moving into an epoch that shows the grand beauty and power of connection.

An open future shows that we can thrive, flourish, innovate, create, evolve, prosper, blossom and go towards our imaginal future, just by taking away the barriers that disconnect us from ourselves and others. There is a future ready and waiting to emerge, and it will more readily do so when the obstacles to connectivity are removed.

People are hardwired for social, cultural and spiritual connection. Barriers that obstruct connection are installed only when survival instincts and the base desire to let self-interests supersede anything else block our more evolved wiring. At one time, impediments to connectivity was the status quo. But as barriers come down, we now see that impedance is not normal, and instead what is normal is our natural ability and desire to commune.

What can help us become more proactive towards making a Quantum Revolution take shape? How can we use and channel our more enlightened aspects? To begin with, you have to know your power. You have the power to change—yourself and the world. You have the power to move past your fear of change, and transform from closed to open. Ultimately, as Franklin Delano Roosevelt said, "The only thing you have to fear is fear itself."

"The first sign of Spirit is courage," the author and former Catholic priest Matthew Fox once said. The act of courage is not as hard as you may think.

It is all about habitual patterning and re-patterning, and the creation of new stories that guide how we move through life. Habits become ingrained the more you practice them—since our prevailing model of life is one that reflects a closed system, that is the habitual pattern and story that people carry with them, and behaviors are accentuated in that way. But as society moves towards an open model, new habits and a new story are being learned. Just by creating new habits, more people are transforming. As you go towards an open and emerging future, your habits will change, if you become more conscious of how you carry yourself.

All it takes is finding the courage to go towards an open future and move beyond the closed parts of yourself. You will never attain perfection, but you can attain your best loving embodiment, and that is good enough.

A Quantum Revolution is not just about personal transformation, although we know that we have to be the change we wish to see in the world. It is about aligning towards the heart of an open culture and feeling yourself as an open vessel; at the same time, it is also about society moving forward towards an open culture—each feeds the other: the personal is the political.

There is a strong transformative energy manifesting—we are moving towards a new, emerging model in society. The open future is taking hold in the mainstream in every realm and is creating a new economic model, as businesses see that embracing an open model can lead to more value for the company.

The companies that are embracing this new model understand that the obligation of business is not to the shareholders but instead to the stakeholders—everyone associated in the success of the business, from customers to employees, suppliers, the environment and investors—and it is these types of businesses that are the ones that will prosper in the new emerging future. By patronizing these businesses, you are showing that you embrace the new open future economic model.

You cannot just sit on your couch and wait for the flowering of this new open future. You have to seize the day—the time is upon us. This will not be a violent revolution, but it is a revolution nonetheless—albeit a nonviolent one. It is a revolution of the mind, body, heart and spirit. We will achieve it by demonstrating our personal power, and we will demonstrate it by moving forward with a big mind and a big heart.

Where does power derive from? Is it something someone—the government, the authorities, the doctors, the lawyers, the politicians, the police, and others—gives you? No, power is never derived from without—it comes from within. Never, ever give your power away, because when you do so you then feel helpless. To empower yourself, bring your power back to yourself.

As we wrap our minds around what is emerging, acting from our power will become the norm—we know it is coming, and we are ready to consciously think, speak and act in a way that furthers this along.

There is much static that comes your way on a daily basis—most of it from the demands of life—and it can disrupt your best intentions. But if you focus your mind on where we are going, and know there is nothing that can ever stop you—you become unstoppable. Your actions and your thoughts will speak the loudest.

If you can let go of dogmas and polemics and embrace the new, you will see the emerging open future. Know there are many who are laying down the tracks of what is new. There have been many people like this who have graced this planet in the past, and there are many more now who are doing so. You can be one of them, just by the way you walk the earth. Live and be as the Spanish proverb that says, "Traveler, roads are made by walking."

How many roads must a man walk down, before you call him a man? The answer my friend (with apologies to Bob Dylan) is not blowing in the wind. The answer is in front of you and me. It's right here and right now. It is in our grasp.

Let's seize the day and continue to create the world we know to be true. There is no other or better way.

Watch: an Interview with Matthew Fox and Adam Bucko, co-authors of the book, *Occupy Spirituality*, from the video interview series, "Interviews with the Leading Edge." http://drmichaelwayne.com/leadingedge/matthew-fox-adam-bucko/

Appendix A:
The Quantum Revolution Acronym

SOCIAL

S: Speed – Ideas spread very fast these days

O: Open – Open systems succeed, closed systems fail

C: Collaboration – Working with others, especially like-minded folks, creates synergy and the potential for Scenius.

I: Individual – It takes the commitment of individuals to make this happen

A: Alignment – You need to be in alignment with your highest Self, and operating from essence, as opposed to ego. Then you are in resonance with the Field.

L: Leadership – It takes leaders, people who have bold visions, have the will to know what they want, and want to make it happen.

Appendix B:
The 50 Components of a Quantum Revolution

1. Living in truth/being in alignment
2. Quantum thinking/quantum consciousness/big mind
3. Vision
4. Leadership
5. Evolutionary spirituality/conscious evolution
6. Going past comfort zones
7. Don't take anything personally
8. Living a Low Density Lifestyle
9. Healing and release
10. Justice and righteousness
11. Presence/awareness/mindfulness
12. Understanding the matrix of how things are connected
13. Intention/commitment/focus
14. Thinking holistically - seeing the parts from the whole: From the One comes the many
15. Seeing with your heart open
16. Resonance - resonance with others of a heart/mind nature
17. Stillness

18. Investment in human capital
19. Collaboration/cooperation
20. Open system
21. Awakened/self-realized/self-actualized/complete human being
22. Accountability
23. Nonviolence/do no harm
24. Passion
25. Taking a stand, be principled
26. Sustainable living/sustainable eating
27. Compassion
28. Beginner's mind
29. Using your innate genius potential
30. The hero's journey
31. Dialoging and understanding another's point of view
32. Questioning assumptions
32. Visual thinking
34. Feeling connected to everyone and everything: Dissolving subject-object duality
35. Dropping baggage
36. Surrender/letting go
37. Formulating the question - the answers are already there, all it takes is figuring out what the question is

38. Nonattachment
39. Connected to the Source, the larger field, the Sacred Mind
40. Freedom - both outer and inner. Outer is not having forces outside of me limit my actions. Inner is having the awakened awareness to be free of habitual ways of thinking and acting that govern our actions
41. Being aware of the shadow side
42. Living in service of our highest goal
43. Think globally, act locally
44. Give love
45. Deep knowing—through deep knowing, the field of the future begins to emerge
46. Don't blame—take ownership of your actions
47. We are all interconnected—we are the 100%
48. Think not in black and white terms, but be a nuanced thinker – there are shades of grey to everything
49. Embrace a democracy that aims to cultivate the greater good
50. Dream big

About the Author

Michael Wayne, Ph.D., L.Ac., is the author of the groundbreaking book, *Quantum-Integral Medicine: Towards a New Science of Healing and Human Potential,* and also *The Low Density Lifestyle.* In addition, he has written a novel, *The Knuckleball From Hell.*

Dr. Wayne has over 25 years experience in the field of Chinese Medicine, and has a private practice as a practitioner of Acupuncture, Chinese Medicine, and Integrative Medicine. His Ph.D. is in the field of Quantum-Integral Medicine—a field he has pioneered—which is about the science of emerging properties, and how it relates to the innate healing system and human potential.

He is also the Producer/Host of the video interview series Interviews with the Leading Edge, at www.LeadingEdgeInterviews.com, and the leader of the Academy for Quantum Revolutionaries, a training program to help people find and access their leading edge, and by doing so, cultivate the power to transform individually and collectively. You can learn more about the Academy at www.QuantumRevolution.net.

Dr. Wayne's work has been publicly praised by Marianne Williamson and Dr. Larry Dossey; Marianne Williamson said of him, *"Michael Wayne has brought us closer to the understanding we need in order to heal ourselves, each other and the world."* And Larry Dossey said, *"A revolution in medicine is taking place, and no one sees this more clearly than Dr. Michael Wayne."*

His work has received national media attention by the likes of *Alternative Medicine, the New York Post, Hay House Radio, Positive Health, Wellbeing Journal, Martha Stewart's Whole Living* and *Acupuncture Today*.

His website is www.DrMichaelWayne.com.

www.ingramcontent.com/pod-product-compliance
Lightning Source LLC
Chambersburg PA
CBHW061259110426
42742CB00012BA/1983